VISIONS OF PURGATORY

A Private Revelation

Originally published as *Regard sur le Purgatoire*, © 1994 by SAINT-PAUL éditions religieuses, 101 rue de Sèvres, lot 1665, 75272 PARIS, cedex 06.

English translation copyright © 2014 by Scepter Publishers, Inc.
P.O. Box 1391
New Rochelle, NY 10802
www.scepterpublishers.org

Text design by Rose Design

Printed in the United States of America

ISBN: 978-1-59417-218-2

VISIONS OF PURGATORY

A Private Revelation

ANONYMOUS

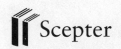 Scepter

"My child, put heaven in your soul,

purgatory in your heart,

and earth in your hands . . .

That is to say: Heaven should be the object of your

contemplation,

purgatory should be the privileged object of your prayer,

earth should be the place where you sanctify yourself

by your works and the accomplishment of your

duties of state."

Contents

PREFACE

Meditating on the mystery of purgatory in the light of the teachings of the Church is a source of great spiritual profit for the Christian. This meditation gives us, in effect, a more profound sense of the holiness of God, as well as a high idea of our vocation, which does not support lukewarmness or cowardly compromises with the world. There we learn purity of love and intensify our desire to see God. Finally, this meditation increases our charity by pushing us to work for those whom St. Veronica Giuliani compassionately calls "the forgotten souls."

Don't they have a right, in fact, to our particular concern by reason of their poverty and their suffering? Doesn't fraternal charity, which Jesus praised with such insistence in the parable of the Good Samaritan, provide us with a pressing duty of hastening their deliverance by prayer and offerings? St. Thérèse of Lisieux was convinced of this; she never missed saying six Our Fathers and six Hail Marys for them every evening. There were many saints throughout the ages who were called to pray especially for the souls in purgatory. The name of St. Catherine of Genoa is noted especially. Her *Treatise on Purgatory* is the admirable summary of a mystical experience or—in some sense—a profound knowledge in the depths of her heart of the suffering that the souls endure in that place of purification.

To encourage the faithful to pray for the souls of purgatory, it seems opportune to publish this book whose author, at the request of his spiritual director, wishes to remain anonymous. Certainly, private revelations do not add anything to the unique revelation of Jesus Christ, which is guarded and transmitted faithfully by the Church. Their conformity with the teaching of the magisterium should be verified.

It should also be noted that the ecclesiastical approval itself, where it is granted, does not guarantee the supernatural origin of what is published here. Finally, it is important to emphasize that private revelations are not intended to satisfy a vain curiosity or to decide problems discussed by theologians. That is to say, the reader of this work is free to make his or her own judgment.

For my part, I would like this account, beyond its particular form, to revive devotion to the souls in purgatory and promote beneficial reflections. With St. Catherine of Genoa, it is good to say:

> O infinite good, how is it that you are not loved and known more by those who are made to know and rejoice in thee? By the little bit of feeling and of taste that God by his grace gives as proof, man should leave this world, to possess them, leaving every other thing.

—*SPIRITUAL DIALOGUE*, PART III

Henri Brincard
Bishop of Puy in Velay, France

INTRODUCTION

The reader will be undoubtedly surprised by the clarity and sobriety of this account of purgatory. One of its principal features is emphasizing the luminous aspect of this mystery. And it is particularly fortunate because, as Cardinal Charles Journet says, "We can take more consolation than fear from purgatory." Purgatory is a gift of the wounded heart of the Lamb, where Mercy envelops Justice. Its contemplation should be a font of acts of thanksgiving and of praise; we should avoid it, not through servile fear, but to "please God," as St. Thérèse of Lisieux tells us.

We would like to make a few comments on this narrative:

To offer our readers teachings that will be of profit to all, we have omitted, with the approval of knowledgeable theologians, anything that could distract one's attention from what is essential. We have also removed passages concerning the personal life of the author, who, by the advice of his spiritual director, prefers to remain anonymous.

The text has been written chronologically. In order to facilitate its understanding, it has been divided into three parts. The first part concerns the purpose of private revelations and the way of gaining profit from them. In the second part, the teachings of a more doctrinal character have been systematically arranged to form, in some way, a treatise on purgatory. The third and final part is dedicated to some manifestations of souls in purgatory. This arrangement does not strictly follow the chronological order of the original account, insofar as it has at times been beneficial to bring together passages on some common theme.

Given the profundity of the published text, it has seemed indispensable to add notes to make some passages clearer. These notes are inspired above all by the teachings of St. Thomas Aquinas.

A NOTE CONCERNING PRIVATE REVELATIONS

The Catholic Church considers private revelations possible and even real in some cases (since it has approved some), but relatively rare and necessarily subject to public revelation.[1]

These private revelations do not add anything to the deposit of Faith, which closed with the death of the last apostle. Actually, "He who gave us his Son, who is the Word, has no other Word to give us: He has told us everything at the same time, once and for all, in this single Word."[2] Private revelations are divided into those that are strictly private, destined for a single believer, and those of a more public character, concerning the life of the Church.[3]

---

[1] *Dictionnaire Apologétique de la Foi,* art. "Revelation," vol. IV [Paris: G. Beauchesne, 1928], col. 1008).

[2] St. John of the Cross, *Subida al Monte Carmelo, II, 20, "Obras Espirituales."*

[3] See René Laurentin, *"Fonction et statut des apparitions,"* in *Vraies et fausses apparitions dans L'Eglise* (Paris: Lethielleux, 1976), 163.

These "public" revelations are useful for the instruction of the faithful about what they have to do "as may be necessary for the salvation of the elect."[4]

The Church does not approve them until they have been carefully investigated, and it makes sure, above all, of the objectivity of the facts and the usefulness of the messages within general revelation. In fact, even if they are approved, they are not an object of faith. However, these "revelations, if they are divine, oblige those to whom they are made and those who are certain of their historical and theological truth" (*Dictionnaire Apologétique*, article cited). On these private revelations "prudence is imposed, but not systematic disparagement nor mocking skepticism."[5]

---

[4] St. Thomas Aquinas, *Summa Theologica* II–II, q. 174–176.
[5] Laurentin, "*Fonction*," 163.

HAVING THE HEART OF A CHILD

Oh Love! what can be said about you?
Those who feel you do not understand you;
those who want to understand you cannot know you.
Oh fire of Love! What are you doing in this man?
You are purifying him as fire purifies gold,
and afterwards you will take him with you to
   your homeland,
to that end for which you have created him.

—St. Catherine of Genoa,
Spiritual Dialogue, Part III

"I WAS IN PRISON AND YOU VISITED ME . . ."

The voice of Jesus made itself heard in my soul, very clearly and intimately:

> *I want you to pray for these holy souls in purgatory, for my divine Heart is burning with love for them.*
>
> *I ardently desire their liberation, to be able to finally unite them to me totally! Pray for them, and write all that will be revealed to you.*
>
> *Do not forget my words: "I was in prison and you visited me."*
>
> *Apply them to these holy souls: it is me that you are visiting in them, with your prayers and your deeds in their favor and for their intentions.*
>
> *Look at their perfection, which should serve as a lesson to you: suffering the most terrible pains, they do not look, however, at their torments, for they are totally abandoned to my Love and to the Will of my Father.*
>
> *Their only concern is our Glory.*
>
> *Learn from these holy souls the purity of love which gazes only at my Heart. Be at peace, my child, and do what I am asking of you.*

What magnificent teaching, what consolation and peace! My God, give me the grace of a wholehearted obedience, trusting and perfect, which will make me not only fulfill, but to get ahead of your desires. Lord, give me light, give me the strength to be faithful to you.

THE ANNOUNCEMENT

During my morning prayer, while I was praying for the souls in purgatory, my guardian angel showed himself to my soul and did so in a completely interior way. On hearing the usual greeting: "Praised be Jesus Christ!" I bowed to respond, and the angel inspired me to raise my head to receive the Sign of the Cross that he traced on my forehead. I was able to look at him, a messenger of divine love enveloped in light, and my soul felt a great peace, a profound joy. His face shone and he looked at me with gentleness and gravity. On seeing the purple belt on his white tunic, I understood what our Lord wanted of me: prayer and penance.

He made me understand how much our Lord loves us, and how he wanted to reveal to every soul the marvels of his Love. Jesus wants from now on to invite me into the light of his heart, to the discovery and contemplation of the mystery of purgatory. I felt a slight anxiety, but the angel calmed me by saying:

Don't be troubled or afraid.

Purgatory is a mystery of love and mercy, and in discovering this, your soul will feel itself called to a greater love for our Lord.

The knowledge of purgatory will bring you great graces of sanctification; it will allow you to

expand your charity and enter more deeply into the
pure Will of God.
   I am at your side to support you; do not have
any fear.

Indeed, is not an angel at our side to sustain us,
guard us, and enlighten our soul? I have nothing to
fear; I just have to dispose myself and surrender myself
to the pure will of God. How little does the rest matter! This is what I told my angel, asking that he help
me and teach me to fulfill better and better what God
wants of me. May Jesus dispose of me as he wishes,
since it's so good that he only reveals his plans for
us little by little. I know that our weakness could not
bear an immediate and total confrontation with the
demands of divine love. . . . Only with the help of
grace and a progressive knowledge that we receive, since
our nature has to be purified without ceasing. And the
angel continued:

Purgatory is a great mystery.
   You will soon learn and discover many things:
some will be very beautiful and consoling, while
others will seem terrible to you.
   However, never forget that, no matter how
rough and painful purgatory seems to you, it is a
mystery of justice as much as of mercy; it is above
all a free gift of love.
   No matter what happens, remain at peace.
   You will have to suffer a lot in order to learn to
love a lot.

You know that Jesus wants to elevate you more and more, from knowledge to knowledge, from love to love, up to his Eucharistic Heart, the font of all love.[1]

Then the angel disappeared from my interior view. I remained with great peace despite these very serious words. But the prospect of having to write everything tormented me. It is another effect of this terrible self-will, which unceasingly acts as a brake on our march toward the Only Good!

THE GUARDIAN ANGEL[2]

I receive purely interior and intellectual lights during my prayer, but my holy guardian angel intervenes sometimes

---

[1] In 1921, at the institution of the Feast of the Eucharistic Heart of Jesus, whose celebration was fixed for the Thursday after the octave of Corpus Christi, Pope Benedict XV said: "By this means, the Church wants to encourage the faithful more strongly to approach with confidence and consume their hearts more and more in the flames of divine charity of the ardent Sacred Heart, when in his infinite love, he instituted the Holy Eucharist, where that same divine Heart guards and loves his faithful, living in them, as they themselves live in Him. In the Sacrament of the Holy Eucharist, he offers and gives himself to us as victim, as a companion, as food, as viaticum and as a pledge of future glory" (November 9, 1921).

[2] God makes use of the faithful angels in the government of his creation and thus the divine truth is manifested to men by means of the angels. This illumination takes place in the order of faith, and in the order of action. St. John of the Cross evoked this ministry of the angels in respect to men. The angels are our shepherds. They not only carry our messages to God, but also bear the messages of God. They nourish our souls with sweet inspirations and divine communications, and like good shepherds, they protect and defend us against the wolves; the demons. By their secret inspirations, they procure for souls a deep knowledge of God, and they make the souls burn in the living flame of their love for him, even to the point of leaving them totally wounded by love for God (opinions and maxims in his *Obras Espirituales*).

in a direct way to point out some details and, above all, to help me to formalize the mysterious realities my intelligence grasps. I perceive the luminous presence of the angel in a distinct way, with the eyes of my soul. It is an image, of course, since it does not have a body[3] and does not appear perceptible to my external gaze. But it is an image that is so clear, so precise, and so evident that I cannot doubt the presence of the one who is communicating with me. It is the presence, not the image, that is important—the communication established between the soul and the divine. God is master of his gifts and uses them for his glory and our sanctification to stimulate faith, hope, and charity in us.

The angel appears almost always in an unexpected way. It would be very dangerous to involve the imagination in an ardent desire to see and understand. Thanks to God, obedience to my spiritual father and the fear that was aroused in me at the beginning by the interventions of the angel have

---

[3] The angel is a spirit; it does not have a body. This spirituality is not a defined dogma of Faith. Father Heris (Charles V. Heris, OP) an eminent Dominican theologian, says: "It would be erroneous, or at least imprudent, to hold that angels have bodies. Or even that they have an ethereal body." The angel created by God is a humble participant in the divine life through the gift of grace. The faithful angel enjoys the glorious vision, that is, the final plenitude of the grace received. When an angel appears, it may be perceptible to one's external gaze, assuming a sensible body that is not alive and only represents its intelligible properties. Then it is a matter of an exterior vision (also called corporal), but the angel can equally become perceptible only in the imagination of the subject: This is an imaginative vision, although it is not perceived by the eyes. It is not proper, in this case, to speak of an imaginary vision. We can also add that the angel is not in a place, but there where it is acting, because it is not subject to a localization of space. We also have to note that it is not really speaking either: it is only producing sounds that are similar to human voices (see Thomas Aquinas, *Summa Theologica* Ia, q. 5).

allowed me to avoid this pitfall. The vision of the angel, centered in the imagination, conceals in some way the intellectual vision and enriches the memory. I have never had an imaginary vision that was not preceded by an intellectual vision of the same reality, since the role of the imaginary vision is secondary; it does not communicate to the imagination, memory, understanding more than what they are incapable of perceiving of the supernatural realities.

The teachings of the angel are above all a call to prayer and a constant interior purification. They fill the soul with peace, with sweetness, increasing one's love and putting one before one's God in a state of increasing humility. God wants this humility and this love, which are so effective during the vision, to be able to be prolonged afterward in daily life. This is the purpose. . . .

THE TEACHING OF THE GUARDIAN ANGEL

When I was meditating about the latest graces I had received, my angel showed himself to me in a very vivid light. This, as always, frightened me in the beginning. He slowly traced a cross on my forehead and said in a serious tone of voice:

> My child, listen to me, and take good note of everything that I am telling you.
>
> The Most High will permit some souls who are still in purgatory to show themselves to you mysteriously.
>
> You have nothing to fear; you only have to humble yourself deeply before the Divine Majesty and put yourself at the service of the Lord.

*These holy souls will not be able to come to
you without divine permission, and they will never
harm you—quite the contrary.*

These words frightened me even more. I asked the
angel how I could tell the difference between the truth and
possible illusions (since the imagination sometimes works
too hard) or manifestations of diabolical origin (since the
devil is always trying to sink souls into uncertainty, doubt,
or error). I also asked him if these manifestations were
indispensable. He answered me kindly:

*If the Most High acts with you in this way, it is for
your benefit and that of the Church; he is making
use of you as a channel: your job is to transmit the
water to your brethren without jealously retaining
it for yourself.*

*Your soul should have a triple disposition: total
submission to the pure will of God, a profound
humility in the presence of these holy souls, and
radical obedience and trust in your Father.*

*God is love; if he allows you to have these graces
it is for your sanctification, to open your soul up to
his infinite love, to saturate it in love for all of your
brethren, and to purify you in the cross of Jesus.*

*Theses graces will be for you an occasion of
suffering as well as deep spiritual joy.*

*Offer everything for these blessed souls in order
to glorify the mercy of God.*

I assented in a prayerful silence. Immediately the angel
continued:

*When any of these blessed souls come, you
will greet them in the name of Jesus; they will
always answer you either through a sign or
by speaking.*

*Sometimes souls will not be able to speak to
you, for they are in the great purgatory; they are
not able to see you.*

*God shows them to you so you can pray for
them.*

*At times, however, they will answer your greet-
ing with "Laudemus Dominum" and make the Sign
of the Cross.*

*Always ask for a sign; this is not impudence but
prudence.*

*Never ask questions of a soul; only God is
the Master of what the soul tells you, if he or she
speaks to you.*

*In these graces of purgatory, you are only asked
for one thing: to love, and, as a consequence, to
pray—which is the same thing.*

*If our Lord opens purgatory to your interior
view, it is to stimulate love in you.*

*If he wants you to write about it, it is to arouse
love in souls.*

Everything is aimed at one single thing: love.

My soul was left with very great peace. I thanked my angel,
who encouraged me with a gesture and concluded:

*If you only knew what love is!
Love is a gift of God because it is God who
gives himself to you.*

Read these passages of Scripture again: "God is love, and he who abides in love abides in God, and God in him."

Often read this verse: it will give you strength, joy, and peace.

If you only knew that you are a child of God— if you were convinced that you are truly the child of Infinite Love!

Let God come to you; let God establish himself in you and communicate with you.

Allow him to pour himself out like a river of fire setting fire to the whole universe!

Be a carrier of this fire of love, of this light!

God is love . . . God is love . . . God is love . . .

The angel was radiant as he said these words, as though in ecstasy as he contemplated the face of this infinite Love. I saw reflected in him the manifestations of divine love and, without realizing it, I knelt before the angel. One cannot imagine what it was like: My soul was enraptured at the sight of this colloquy of love between love itself and his messenger, and I felt included in that interchange of love, which was gracious and ineffable. I cannot explain it, but as he sang the praises of divine love, the angel communicated that love to me. My soul was submerged in love.

SOME IMAGES TO HELP YOU UNDERSTAND

During the evening, I asked myself: What was happening to allow me to perceive so much concerning this great mystery of purgatory? At that moment my angel showed himself to the eyes of my soul, radiant and smiling. The precious purple-colored cross he wore was radiant. He put his hand on my arm and said to me gently:

> *My child, those images are destined to make you understand spiritual realities which you cannot penetrate on your own.*
>
> *The All Powerful wants to make use of all the riches of your imagination to allow you to enter more and more deeply into these mysteries.*

These explanations were very surprising to me, and my soul became anxious. *What if all of this is my imagination, or just an illusion?* I thought. I began to be seized by fear. Then the angel spoke to me reassuringly.

> No, *my child, they are not illusions.*
>
> *Since when are imaginary visions an illusion?*
>
> *They are simply a way of knowing that our Lord concedes to souls, and it is important not to deform them, nor adorn or change them in human ways.*
>
> *Therefore, I always ask that you note down everything that you have seen and heard, and that you do it immediately after having received these graces. Don't let time pass for fear that human thoughts may be mixed up with God's gift.*
>
> *Remain in the peace of Jesus Christ.*

Having said this the angel smiled and disappeared. My soul remained calm and peaceful.

THE IMAGINATION AT THE SERVICE OF THE INTELLIGENCE

While I was working in the garden, my guardian angel showed himself to my internal view, appearing in a dazzling light so vivid that it transformed everything, pulling me with force and removing from my sight all that was not in this light. He said to me: "Praised be Jesus Christ."

I was speechless with surprise, but I tried to convince myself that it was nothing more than an illusion. Then, without saying anything, the angel approached me and traced the Sign of the Cross on my forehead with his thumb. He always did this, but this time it was really special: He pressed so strongly that I jumped back. He continued in a tranquil voice:

Since when are imaginary visions an illusion?

Confused, I stood there without being able to say anything; the cross on my forehead hurt. At least that sensation was not an illusion! The angel continued in a grave tone:

Good, I have to explain to you what an imaginary vision is, and you will write it down, and read it again from time to time, and also you will transmit it to your spiritual Father.

My God! It seems as if I wanted to remove myself from your will, but in your infinite tenderness toward me, you have sent your angel to remind me that it is not my will that matters, but yours. How miserable I am. . . . Then I told the angel, who was praying in silence while I raised my soul toward our Lord:

Praised be Jesus Christ! Most holy angel, be for me a bringer of light and the infinite love of God, whom you have the grace of contemplating without ceasing.

On hearing these words, which came from my heart more than from my mouth, and under the effect of a deep interior impulse, my angel, even more resplendent with light, prostrated himself deeply, with his face in his hands, saying:

> *Adoration, praise, honor, and glory*
> *to our thrice Holy God,*
> *our Creator and your Father!*

Then he slowly arose, crossed his hands over his breast, and continued with his teaching.

> *Seeing and understanding are one and the same thing in God. Imaginary visions are nothing other than a means granted to the soul by the Lord, which makes it capable of understanding what it needs to know. God infuses a light in the intelligence, and the soul perceives this light as an intellectual vision. It often cannot be understood nor translated into a communication that other souls can receive as a message or see as a teaching.*
>
> *It happens then that our Lord wants to make it possible that this light—infused into the intelligence and perceived by the soul as an intellectual vision—be understood and communicated. Then he himself sketches in the imagination images that*

change this light into a sensible power, which the
soul can understand and describe. It is not the
imaginary vision; you can see that there is nothing
of a phantasm here.

I listened to this explanation with great interest and attention. I asked my angel to explain how he was visible to my
interior sight. He told me:

We angels, as you know, do not have a body, and
therefore you cannot see us as we really are; we
show ourselves as images perceptible to your inte-
rior senses, images that cover and manifest in some
way our presence near you.

The saints show themselves in this same way,
as do the poor souls in purgatory. Your eyes cannot
see them, and yet nevertheless they really exist.

When our Lord wants them to appear to you,
he infuses in your intellect the deep reality of their
presence and sees that they manifest this presence
in a sensible way, imprinting their image in your
imagination.

In your spiritual life it is very important
that your imagination be constantly purified and
tamed—it should be the servant of the intellect.
But the imagination is a vagabond and often finds
an accomplice in the memory; the memory is a
glutton, which swallows all the imagination pres-
ents to it. These two powers are very versatile;
they love to operate independently of the will and
the intellect.

However, they should submit.

When you have visions of this kind, you should only pay attention to them if they bring you lights that allow you to understand better what our Lord is giving to you in an intellectual vision. God gives these graces for the growth of the soul in knowledge and love; one shouldn't overestimate them, but it would be foolish to despise them. They are a gift of God.

Always look toward the Giver; the gift that he presents you with in his mercy should always make you turn to him.

After ending his teaching, the angel slowly crossed his hands and placed them over the cross that adorned his radiant tunic. He bowed in silent adoration of God and then disappeared from my interior view.

THE GREAT HOPE

Evening prayer. My soul was totally absorbed by contemplation of the mystery of the Eucharistic Heart of Jesus, when suddenly I saw a multitude of persons who seemed submerged in a great fire; they were praying intensely. I understood that I was being shown the souls in purgatory. . . . Then our Lord let me hear his voice in my soul:

My child, pray for these souls in order to bring closer the moment when they will be perfectly united to me.

Their union in this time of purgatory is only in the desire that they have of me—a desire that burns like a fire.

*Their prayers are hope, because it is there in
purgatory where this virtue develops in its purity
and perfection.*

*Purgatory is the great mercy of my Eucharistic
Heart. The greatest purification for a soul is the
desire that they have for me, the desire that my
Eucharistic Heart ignites in your hearts; it is all
hope when I put it in your souls.*

*In this time that is coming, the fire will burn
many souls with the desire of possessing me that
I will place in them. My Church will know this
burning of desire for me, and souls will learn hope
passing through this trial of love. . . .*

The Lord then touched my soul with a dart of brilliant fire
from his divine heart, and as I fainted beneath the gentle
burning—like an arrow of fire—he told me with infinite
gentleness:

*Oh, little soul! I want to burn you with this desire,
because this desire that you have for me calls me to
unite with you.*

I cannot describe the delights that then filled my soul: I was
as if submerged in the love of the Eucharistic Heart, the
divine Heart of Jesus—suffering cruelly for not being able
to love him perfectly and nevertheless filled with an ineffable happiness. What happiness, then! Oh, infinite love!

THE MEANING OF THE GRACES YOU RECEIVE

Upon finishing my evening prayers, my guardian angel
appeared before me. A cross of red fire adorned his tunic

with an unsustainable brightness, vivid red as blood. I understood that I should intensify my prayer and prepare myself for new sufferings. He said to me:

> *Praised be Jesus Christ!*
> *Someone very close to you is still in purgatory; pray and ask for prayers for his liberation. The Most Blessed Virgin wants this very much.*
> *If she could, she would empty the whole of purgatory all at once. If you pray and offer sacrifices, this soul will be freed on Good Friday.*

These words greatly disturbed me; this seemed so close to me and so far away at the same time. But the fact is that time does not exist after death—at least not as we understand it here.[4] I asked the angel if this man had to suffer a lot and what I should do. The angel answered me:

---

[4] From the time that the soul is separated from the body, it is no longer submitted to continuous time: it is immutable in its will, which leads it toward the final end that it has chosen. In fact, it knows a duration without changes nor succession; a perpetual present, which the theologians call "aeviternity." Nevertheless, the thoughts and affections of the separated soul succeed each other, and the measure of this succession is "discrete time." Each thought lasts for an instant, which does not correspond with continuous time. Consequently the soul knows a double duration: that of eternity and that of "discontinuous" time. Aeviternity is distinguished from eternity not only because it has a beginning, but also because it is associated with "discontinuous time." When the soul enters into the beatific vision, it participates in the eternity of God. This participated eternity is distinguished from the "essential" eternity of God, because it does not measure in the glorified soul anything other than the beatific vision and the vision of God, which is what gives origin to it. Let us remember that in God eternity is a result of his absolute immutability: Because God is his being and he himself is his eternity, he has neither beginning nor end; he exists all at once without knowing any succession.

*Yes, he suffers a lot, more and more, because he is
close to his liberation. But it is a suffering of love,
as you already know. Pray, offer your Masses for
him, and say often, "Oh, my beloved and good
Jesus," especially after receiving Communion.
Above all, do penance!*

*Fasting and penance are great resources for
the blessed souls in purgatory. But for these
mortifications you should ask the permission of
your Father . . .*

*Mortify your senses, especially your eyes and
your tongue, for God needs interior and silent
souls. Keep your pains and sorrows only for Jesus;
don't talk about them to anyone but him.*

*Don't cause burdens for your brothers. You
should be a joyful soul on the cross. And now that
you know the faults of this soul, make reparation
by exercising the opposite virtues, so that they will
be reversed, if one may say that. . . .*

I saw this person in the midst of some clear flames. I
told my angel that sometimes I didn't know what to do,
because I was afraid of making a mistake, or of being
a victim of my imagination. The angel looked at me
severely, and this person did, too, and then this person
said to me firmly:

*Good! You know what you should do. You should
love much, pray a lot, be quiet about the gifts of
God, and before all else, be obedient to your father
[spiritual director].*

Don't give in to discouragement!
So that your reluctance may not be prejudicial
to us, we need your prayers and your help—for
ourselves but above all for God.
Since it is a duty for you, it will glorify God.

This admonition shook me and at the same time tranquilized me. And the person continued with great firmness and gentleness.

You should not ask anything. God knows what he
is doing in you. . . .
Surrender yourself and let him do in you by
grace whatever he wants.
He is giving you these graces so that you com-
municate them to the Holy Church.
God wants to use these graces for good, to
awaken sleeping souls, to tell men who are enclosed
in egoism that their lives do not end here on earth
but will develop fully after their bodily death.
These days very few think of purgatory; they
almost doubt its existence, as they do in regard to
hell. It is up to you to say that heaven, purgatory,
and hell exist!
Yes, hell exists—and unfortunately it is not empty.

For a moment I saw this mystery of hell. I thought I would die from the sight. I will not say anything more. My angel sustained me and continued speaking:

God, who is all Goodness, has nevertheless wanted
to make known this great mystery of the purgatory
of his love. Various saints, instructed by divine

*wisdom and filled with the light of its truth, have
taught and written about this mystery of love, to
glorify the Lord in his mercy, to enlighten souls and
warn them, to arouse in the Holy Church more
prayers and suffrages in our favor.*

The person became quiet, raised his eyes radiantly to
heaven, and then continued speaking gravely.

*Listen well to what I tell you. It is the very reason
for the graces you are receiving. God gives them
to you generously, in spite of your unworthiness,
because he has had pity on your misery.*

*Contemplating the great mystery of God's
mercy and justice and the final realities should
stimulate you and other souls to holiness, as you
prepare yourself to enter into the House of God
when you die here below.*

*It is meant to stimulate you to holiness—that is
the reason that you are being given these graces. It
is the reason you are being given all these teachings
so abundantly.*

*Yes, you are to be a saint! God wants you to be
a saint; therein is your true happiness.*

*Know how to use all the means Jesus gives you
in the Church—take advantage of them!*

*All of this is being shown to you so that souls
will be inflamed with love—so they will consume
themselves for God, having no other desire than
just doing his will.*

*Do everything to avoid purgatory—not out of
fear, but out of love.*

Pray for us who did not know enough to avoid it. Without choosing anyone in particular—other than those for whom you have an obligation to pray—entrust everything to the Mother of all goodness, the heavenly Treasurer: she will distribute the suffrages according to the will of God.

I am going to tell you the most effective means to avoid going to purgatory. Seek only one thing in everything: the glory of God. Be perfectly free of affection for all creatures and only want to do the will of God.[5] Dispose yourself to die with love. Exercise the virtues of obedience, humility, discretion, and wear the scapular of the Queen of Carmel.

As a matter of fact, this constitutes the program of your life here below.

You should read some good teachings about purgatory to understand it. But who is going to take the time for this nowadays?

Do you know that there is a form of spiritual gluttony that consists in reading only what brings the soul consolation and sensible pleasure?

Many pious persons do not want to read anything except what they like under the pretext that this is what is best for them.

But what they like is not very often the best, and in giving oneself spiritual pleasure in that way, one rapidly falls into complacency.

---

[5] The pure will of God, a frequent expression in these writings, means the design of God's love for each of his creatures.

He stopped speaking and smiled at me. I had never read anything except the *Treatise on Purgatory* by St. Catherine of Genoa, and I understood that this was one of the good teachings to which this person alluded. Then everything disappeared from my sight.

THE INFERNO

In the inferno, the soul finds itself suddenly immersed in an absolute solitude—a density of chaos, death, and nothing. There is no presence, no communication, no love. It is the total absence of movement and desire, an immersion in sin in its brute state, an immersion in absolute, objectified evil. The soul knows itself to be a sinner, but sin no longer belongs to it; it is no longer its own; it possesses one, impregnates one, transfixes one. The soul knows itself to be condemned and sees itself transformed into its own sin. The condemned person and sin are somehow intertwined. This is hell, and it is difficult to explain it. It might be compared to a kind of atomization, or a terrible concentration of evil. Since hell is not a vacuum, it is filled with nothingness. There is an incredible pressure, a density, and a horrible opacity. When I speak of nothingness, I don't mean "not being"—instead, it is the opposite of being, the opposite of love.

In this state the soul does not feel anything; it does not experience anything in its senses. This is a thousand times worse than a known suffering. It is an agony of the soul that knows it is not open to anything else except itself. The spirit is carried into union with the infinite offense (which is sin) with which it has been identified and assimilated more and more. Nevertheless there is no movement, nor progress.

In addition there is no communication among the condemned who are juxtaposed together, overwhelmed by the mere fact of being there. It is worse than hatred, which is a passionate, pulsating movement; instead, this is non-love in its frozen objectivity. Although one burns in hell, one is also submerged in the icy cold of the second death, eternal death. It is non-life: there is no dynamism, no creativity, no evolution. It is a permanent state of vertigo and oppression, which increases without ceasing and keeps intensifying. This death is infinite, and hell is infinite.

This suffering is more atrocious than anything else. The fire that burns here is ice in comparison to hell, just as the most biting cold here is nothing compared to that of the second death. It is not an experience of *not being*, but of *not being what one is*, the absolute impossibility of becoming what one has been called to be in the mystery of the saving cross, since one has despised the free gift of salvation.

OH JESUS, ALL FOR THEM!

My soul was still under the impact of the vision of purgatory that was shown to me yesterday, and I was praying for the holy souls, above all today on the feast of the Expectation of the Virgin Mary.[6] In the light of this

---

[6] The Feast of the Expectation of the Blessed Virgin Mary is very ancient; it probably goes back to the period of the Council of Ephesus and commemorates the divine maternity of the Most Blessed Virgin. It is celebrated on December 18 [in Spain and some other places]. The particular or ecumenical councils, up until Vatican II, have constantly revised the annual feasts, expressions of Christian love. In this book we make allusion to some of these feasts.

feast, I offered God the calm expectation of his Mother in favor of these poor souls who are consumed in such a painful waiting. In effect, just as God was glorified by Mary's calm and trusting waiting, so he is glorified by the waiting of the souls in purgatory, although in a different way. Our Lady has the role of interceding for them. This intention occupies a great part of my day, but the closeness of Christmas fills my soul with peace, joy, strength, and confidence. As evening fell, my holy angel appeared. He said to me encouragingly:

> *In these days of Christmas, you will not see purgatory any more.*
>
> *This should incite you to a greater faithfulness in your prayers in favor of the souls in purgatory.*
>
> *When looking at them, let your soul direct to the Almighty this simple supplication: "My God, everything for them."*[7]
>
> *Steep yourself well in the meaning of these words; say them with faith and love, and do not forget that an abundance of words are not needed to express your charity.*
>
> *Understand well that it is important for you to pray for the souls in purgatory!*
>
> *It is one of your duties of charity, and if you fail in this duty to God, you will be severely punished.*

---

[7] An exclamation of St. Veronica Giuliani: "Oh purgatory, you are very dear to me, pain of the senses, pain of obstacle ("temporal" privation of the vision of God), this pain that surpasses any pain, I want to suffer it all for you, and for the abandoned souls" (*Journal*, selected pages, translated from the Italian by Father Desiré des Planches OMC [Gembloux: Duculot, 1931], 294).

There are many souls who are in purgatory making expiation for not having prayed for the departed ones who were close to them.

The angel became silent. With a gesture of his hand, he showed me purgatory in a very quick, dense vision, and then began speaking again:

How can you remain insensitive to such great suffering of love?

You are on earth, but you participate in the communion of saints;

Is it that you don't have the possibility of going to the intercession of the blessed ones and especially to that of the Mother of God?

Do they cease to pray for you for a single instant, obtaining graces and lights for you?

Well, then, the souls in purgatory also need intercessors, and they find them among you as well as in heaven.

Pray for them; they need your suffrages, and they expect your faithfulness and gratitude. God wants it that way, because your prayers for these blessed souls are an act of charity, a testimony of love which will make you progress in this virtue of the faith, which expands the horizons of your charity and deepens your faith, which enriches and consolidates your hope.

All of this glorifies God and consoles the holy souls in purgatory.

I prayed in silence, repeating without stopping the invocation: "Oh Jesus, all for them, all for these holy souls!" The angel, nodding his approval, told me:

> *The Lord wants you to write all of this for his glory, so that the fire of his charity is extended over the whole earth.*
>
> *All of this will be useful for a great number of souls. To many of your brethren on earth who will read it, our Lord will show his love even more, since there is no one who can remain insensible before so much pain.*
>
> *If souls read this with faith and trust, they will be comforted and will grow in faith, hope, and charity.*
>
> *A great number of souls in purgatory will benefit from the suffrages of prayers and good works that will be done by your brothers who are moved by their sufferings and needs.*
>
> *Do you understand now why you have to write?*
>
> *You should dedicate yourself totally to the service of God who wants to make use of you as of a hidden instrument in the hollow of his hand.*

Upon hearing these words, I had a brief moment of panic. The angel concluded calmly without seeming to notice:

> *Remain in peace! In the peace of God, and not that of the world, which is no more than a caricature and a simulation of the authentic peace of God.*

Remain in faithful obedience to your spiritual director. Open your soul to him, close your ears to the vain noises of the world.

Remain in the secret of God, not counting for anything in the eyes of the world. God is the only one who judges rightly; the world only approves those who adulate it and condemns those who despise it.

Remain in the most pure Heart of Mary, your Immaculate Mother. In her there is nothing but truth and light, and she will open to you the Eucharistic Heart of her Divine Son.

After this the angel left. I am at peace.

PART
2

"Blessed are the clean of heart,
for they shall see God."

—Matthew 5:8

"Love is repaid with love."

—St. John of the Cross

God's mercy upon purgatory

After my prayer, I contemplated our Lord's infinite mercy poured out upon the holy souls in purgatory who are suffering the torments of love. First I saw the loving gaze of the Most Blessed Trinity toward these souls, from the antechamber of heaven to the lowest depths of the great purgatory.[1] I saw how they looked at each soul individually; I saw how the Father contemplated them resplendent in the blood of his Son, the unique and precious price of his or her salvation; he looked at them and loved them infinitely in his crucified and glorious Son.

I saw the Word's gaze resting on the souls in purgatory. He rejoiced to see them submerged in the pure will of God, in a total consent to the love of the Father, and he loved them for the Father, who is also our Father. I saw the Holy Spirit, the Spirit of love, looking at these holy souls with an infinite satisfaction and pouring himself into them fully as into vessels of divine love. It was marvelous. My guardian angel appeared and said:

My child, these holy souls in purgatory are the most beloved sons and daughters of the divine mercy.

They are destined to be eternal jewels of the heavenly Jerusalem, jewels of the Immaculate Spouse. Therefore, they have to be perfectly

---

[1] These terms will be explained in the following pages.

pure; they are totally expiating the slightest sin, the most minute fault, and the slightest shadow is disappearing from them. For this reason these daughters and sons of mercy are exposed to the rigors of divine justice.

I felt a great joy on hearing these words of consolation. The angel prayed at my side for the souls in purgatory, inviting me to imitate him. After a few minutes he told me:

In purgatory the souls know their faults; they have a full perception of them. Through having seen them at the moment of the particular judgment, afterward they have them present in their spirit, but in a general and confused way. They are not to think of them; they adore the divine mercy and glorify the Most Holy Trinity with love and gratitude.

You know that purgatory was created by mercy—the souls are in purgatory by a decree of mercy and the pure gratuity of divine love. For these pains, no matter how terrible they are, are very slight in relation to the infinite offense that sin constitutes.

After this I saw myriads of angels in heaven who were praying for the souls in purgatory, and thousands of saints surrounding the Virgin Mary. My soul rejoiced with consolation. I also saw the prayer that the Church on earth sends up in favor of these souls; it appeared like an abundant rain collected by the angels in cups of gold and presented to the Most Blessed Virgin who offers them to the Divine Trinity. Our Lord blesses this prayer that the angels pour out upon purgatory in such a pure and comforting dew. My guardian angel said to me:

> *That great mystery of the communion of saints and its efficacy in purgatory are also an effect of divine mercy. God gives to the angels and saints of heaven—as well as to those who are still here below—the task of praying for these holy souls and thus giving them some relief. It is a duty for you, a work of mercy in favor of these souls.*

He helped me to understand that the souls in purgatory sometimes receive, according to the plans of Divine Providence, the possibility of showing themselves here on earth. These manifestations can take various forms. In regard to that, the angel told me:

> *These manifestations are also permitted by divine mercy.*
>
> *For the Church militant they have a threefold purpose: to remind the people of God that they should pray for these souls, to remind the people of God to do penance for their sanctification, and to remind the people of God that they are only on earth for a time.*
>
> *These souls sometimes have a knowledge of the future which the Almighty gives them in certain circumstances, and on occasion they can let you know this future which concerns you, offering you signs that will strengthen your faith and also guard, warn, and protect you. You should give thanks for these messengers of mercy and pray for them.*

Oh Lord my God, how many graces and effects of your merciful love! The angel concluded in a more serious way:

> *There are persons who, because they are more excitable or more impressionable, cannot hear the squeaking of a piece of furniture, the creaking of the floor, or the rustling of a curtain without imagining that the souls in purgatory want to communicate something to them. Then, instead of praying for those souls, they seek to enter into communication with them. This is a waste of time, and also a sin—a sin of curiosity and of presumption.*
>
> *One has to be prudent in this area, because there are many abuses and many errors. The mystery of purgatory is not a game; it is a great mystery of divine love.*

Wrapped in a vivid light, he disappeared from my sight after saying these words. I continued my prayer.

ON THE MYSTERY OF PURGATORY

During my morning prayer, there appeared to me an immense, silent, and unmoving fire, with an intense heat. This heat was inconceivable—I was in a bath of fire; my soul burned within and without. I understood that I was being shown the mystery of purgatory.

First there is the fire of love, ignited by God, a fire which is a manifestation of purgatory. This mystical fire seemed to me at the same time both material and spiritual. The mystery of purgatory is that souls are purified in these flames. It is the reparation they owe to God for the remains of sin in them, as well as for the consequences of sin outside of them, throughout all of creation. However, there is no sin in the souls in purgatory—just the remains.[2]

---

[2] Sin is a disorder that offends God, for it is an outrage against his dignity as infinite Good and Creator; the more or less great disorder of sin determines its gravity. We have to distinguish between mortal and venial sin. If man turns away fully from God, he has lost his orientation toward him and by this has lost divine life. A mortal sin is one where man prefers a finite good to infinite divine charity. The turning away from God is accompanied by a disordered attachment to changeable goods, which sin takes as an end that takes the place of God. However, if a man takes a perishable good as his end and uses it without preferring it to God, he commits a venial sin. The disorder is then in the means, and not in the end (*Summa Theologica* I–II, q. 88. a1).

What are the consequences of mortal and venial sin? Well, in mortal sin, man loses his spiritual life and stains his soul, which remains marked by a shameful stain; a grave disorder and an inclination toward evil acts is introduced within his faculties. If the sinner obtains pardon in the sacrament of penance, he recovers the life of grace; his guilt is erased, the blot or stain disappears through the influence of the splendor of grace which once more is exercised upon his soul and which comes from union with God. Mortal sin implies a disordered attachment to perishable goods: it engenders in the soul a disposition or habit if the sin was repeated. This inclination to the disordered pursuit of the sensible good remains, although weakened, after the sin is erased. It is the remains of the absolved sin. Certainly this bad inclination is not dominant; it only exists in the sinner as a habit, unless a very vivid contrition, like that of Mary Magdalene, whose example is cited by St. Thomas, or by the offering of repeated satisfactions, erases it definitively. If that is not the case, these defective dispositions disappear after death. . . . Are they erased in the light of the particular judgment itself, or in purgatory? Opinions differ. St. Thomas writes in his *Commentary on the Sentences:* "The rigor of the punishment corresponds in a real way to the gravity of the sin in the subject" (Fr. Reginald Garrigou-Lagrange, *La vida eterna y la profundidad del alma* [*Life Everlasting and the Immensity of the Soul*], [Madrid: Rialp, 1960], 276).

If one distinguishes the remains of sin from the obligation of punishment resulting from forgiven but not expiated sins, these words of St. Thomas simply mean that the more strongly an inclination is in the soul of the sinner, the longer will be the punishment destined to expiate it. The

The reparation consists in a terrible punishment: to be deprived of God, the temporary privation of the beatific vision. It is a state of unparalleled suffering, a terrible expiation for a soul that is perfectly purified and embraced by divine charity, totally committed to love, which possesses it, attracts it, and wants to give itself in plenitude, when it can still neither grasp nor possess it fully.

My soul felt as though it were torn apart by this suffering. It is a very painful languor of love, an exile far away from the Beloved, a devouring desire to possess the Beloved. It is a waiting inflicted by one's own conduct, thus reaching the Beloved but not being prepared. . . . In purgatory the soul cannot make any progress. It finds itself fixed in the state of waiting, burning with love, subject to the sole will of the Beloved. It is a burning desire that burns without being consumed, an expiatory pain that one is so thankful for. Oh! How thankful!

The punishment of purgatory is to be deprived of God. The soul suffers this deprivation in three painful ways. First, dazzled by the divine light, it is nevertheless still in obscurity; second, attracted by divine love, it is still distanced from that love; and third, captivated by the beauty

---

obligation of the punishment is like rust, says St. Catherine of Genoa, which is consumed by the fire of purgatory and frees the soul from the debt contracted by sin. The sufferings that constitute the pain of purgatory purify the soul not of its defective inclinations but of the debt of his sin (*Summa Theologica*, q. 70, a. 7; St. Catherine of Genoa, *Treatise on Purgatory*, no. 4, pp. 33–34). What is affirmed various times in the text accords perfectly with the interpretation of St. Thomas.

and holiness of God, it feels itself depressed. These three pains are common to all who are in purgatory, and from these come all the others, with variations more or less painful according to each one. Each soul has its own peculiar experiences: remorse for the graces not taken advantage of or squandered; suffering from being forgotten and separated from relatives still on earth; anxious hope for one's liberation from purgatory without any idea when this might occur.

This penalty of separation from God is the state of purgatory, and from it come all the other expiatory sufferings: objective, purifying sufferings that are works of justice. This state is transitory; some day this fire will be put out, and the souls know this. They are in the perfection of hope, entirely on fire with love. . . .

As I prayed, this intellectual vision suddenly ended.

PURGATORY'S FIRE OF LOVE

Silent prayer. From the Eucharistic Heart of Jesus, launching darts of love, I have been given an experience of the fire of purgatory. The fire of purgatory is a fire of love: "Love is as strong as death," and its darts are the flaming darts of God. Purgatory is a fire of love, coming forth from the heart of God, captivating the soul and inflaming it with the desire for the beatific vision. . . . I saw this fire of purgatory ignited in souls—in their interior—by the love of God. The divine love burns; it sears the souls with love for him.

This fire is terrible because it is a fire of love: the love of God ignites in the souls in purgatory a vivid desire for

God. The soul then carries this lighted fire inside itself for God; it is inflamed and turned toward God. The soul is captivated by him and inflamed with a desire for the beatific vision, which is union with God. And it is from this fire of love that all the other pains come—they are recapitulated in it. This fire is so terrible that fire on earth, by comparison, is a gentle ointment. And it provokes in the souls in purgatory an atrocious thirst, so great is its vehemence.

> *My soul thirsts for thee; my flesh faints for thee,*
> *as in a dry and weary land where no water is.*[3]

One can see in this verse of Psalm 63 a metaphor that expresses our desire for God, a desire we experience here below. But my angel did not interpret it in that way. Instead he asked me whether I believed that here on earth many souls were so advanced in love that they were able to apply those words of Scripture to themselves. I saw that it is easier to apply them to the souls in purgatory, since I myself am sadly too far from feeling that thirst for God to recognize myself in those lines.

The souls in purgatory always are attracted forcefully to God, whose love they are experiencing. His love burns them with desire, like a blazing fire that penetrates to the marrow of their soul—and at the same time they are kept in purgatory to expiate their faults and pay their debts, which are the penalties of sin that still remain in them. This expiation itself is loved and

---

[3] Psalm 63:1.

desired—regardless of how painful it might be—because it is the way of reaching union with God. The souls in purgatory have no other will but that of God's, and at the same time they hate sin because the penalties of sin impede this union.

The only way of reaching union with God is to overcome any obstacles in the soul, and in purgatory this is only possible through restorative atonement. This is how the souls who yearn ardently for their union with God will find themselves purified of the penalty of sin and able to enter into the beatific vision. This is the only desire of the souls of purgatory, a desire that is at the same time excited and unsatisfied. It is this opposition that burns them like fire; this is the fire of purgatory. It is a temporary barrier that prevents them from answering their vehement desire to see God fully and to see that union consummated in glory. In this state the soul frequently cries out: "You are just, oh Lord, and your judgments are right!"

The desire of the souls in purgatory is a desire of total conformity to the pure will of God. Entirely turned toward God, the soul no longer has a will of its own, nor looks upon itself or upon others. Everything in the soul is purified, united by the conformity of its will with the will of God, and its gaze is solely on God.

It was as if I had been able to experience a little of the burning fire of purgatory, but there was something else, too—a real fire, almost material, that presents an analogy with our fire on earth, although this fire is different, incomparably more fiery and terrible, and very mysterious. My guardian angel confirmed this intuition to me, telling me that one can see its material character by seeing the material effects it produces.[4]

I have seen this fire as a kind of burning shadow. It was a reddish color and very dark, since purgatory is a dark place in comparison with the ineffable and radiant light

---

[4] In regard to the pains of purgatory, faith is not committed more than on certain points. There are pains of purgatory that are purifying and will end after the final judgment. The principal pain of purgatory is privation of the vision of God. There is also is a secondary pain, that of the senses. "What is its nature? The tradition of the Latin Church, with some exceptions, affirms the purification of souls by a physical fire after life on this earth. The tradition of the Eastern Church is not unanimous on this point, and inclines more in favor of a spiritual fire. The Council of Florence (1438) did not pronounce on this, the object of vivid controversy between Greeks and Latins" (*Dictionnaire de Théologie Catholique*, vol. 5, article *Fire*, cols. 2246–2261). According to St. Robert Bellarmine, the doctrine according to which the souls are purified in purgatory by a physical fire is a *"sentencia probabilisima."* How can the soul, separated from the body, be tormented by a physical fire? St. Thomas Aquinas has dealt with this difficult question with his customary penetration (see *Summa Theologica*, Supplement, q. 70 ter., a. 3). This is the explanation: Fire, by its natural power, cannot reach the soul separated from the body. Indeed, for a body to be able to act upon a spirit, it has to be united to it:

- As the form is united to matter, forming a single composition; this is the case of the soul and the body. But we have to point out that the fire does not cause a sensible suffering in the soul, but a spiritual suffering by holding it captive. The pain of the senses is not the same in this life as in the other. Here it is caused by material agents; in the next life, it is caused by a fire that ignites a spiritual pain.

- As the instrument is united to that which is moved by it. But the fire is not naturally united to the soul separated from the body, neither in the first way nor in the second. It remains, then, that divine justice gives a power of detention to the fire. By virtue of an action of God that makes the fire an instrument of his justice, the fire retains the soul, making use of it, in some form, as a dwelling place; preventing the exercise of its will; preventing it from acting as it wants and where it wants. Certainly the fire is apprehended by the soul as evil, and it causes it a spiritual suffering.

of paradise. In comparison with hell, though, purgatory is very bright, because hell is a reign of eternal darkness (although there, too, a fire burns). . . .

The fire of purgatory imprisons the soul but at the same time surrounds it and envelops it in such a way that the soul finds itself held captive in this material fire. For the soul, this is a great pain and humiliation. . . . Purely spiritual but imprisoned by this material fire, the soul finds itself restricted from its normal spiritual activities, and in this way it submits to the divine will that is manifested in this surprising form of material fire. I believe that there is a double fire: the interior fire of love ignited in the soul by God, and also a true exterior fire, which is a manifestation of the former.

I also think that the fire of purgatory and the fire of hell are the same fire, but I don't know why it is positive, purifying, and ignites love in purgatory, while in hell it is negative, punishing, and arouses hatred.[5] All of this may seem incredible. I am writing as my angel told me; if I am mistaken, it is because I understood poorly. Purgatory is such a great mystery! I submit all of this to Holy Mother the Church, who knows and judges.

THE PAINS OF PURGATORY

Evening prayer. The Lord wanted me to see and understand the pains of purgatory. It is certain that here below we cannot understand exactly what they are like without experiencing them. One can, nevertheless, receive from

---

[5] For St. Thomas Aquinas, the fire of purgatory is substantially the same as that of hell, but its effects in purgatory are different.

God the grace of a real approximation of this mystery in order to give his brothers and sisters a lesson that will stimulate their compassion and prayer in favor of the blessed souls in purgatory.

I saw that in purgatory there is only a single punishment: the privation of the vision of God. All other privations are simply different forms derived from this.[6] This punishment is so harsh because the soul is strongly attracted by God; it desires and goes toward him in a vivid impulse, yet remains paralyzed. The soul experiences the necessity of remaining immobile, in spite of the attraction of love that is driving it.

One can understand this by the fact that the soul, in purgatory, only desires the glory of God. It has cast itself into purgatory, propelled by its love for holiness and the justice of God, and it places God's glory above its own interests. The soul that finds itself in purgatory loves this suffering, which reveals the holiness of God in the mystery of justice. It prefers it a thousand times over an encounter with God that would satisfy its own interests. The suffering of purgatory is terrible; it is a torment of love like nothing else on earth. One could compare it somewhat with the immense suffering of the paralytic at the pool of Bethsaida who only wanted to enter the water when it was agitated but was not able to do so.[7]

---

[6] There are in purgatory two classes of punishment: a) the punishment of not enjoying the vision of God, improperly called the punishment of privation, because one must not confuse it with what the condemned suffer in hell, and b) the pain of the senses, about whose nature the Church has not pronounced in an explicit and solemn form.

[7] See John 5:2–7.

Such is the terrible punishment of purgatory—a heart-rending and ardent languishing of love in the soul. All the rest are nothing more than consequences of this languishing of love: the feeling of estrangement, being forgotten, darkness, hunger for God, the duration of this punishment, the forgetfulness or negligence of those who are still on earth, the clear vision of sin and sadness for having sinned, etc. My angel explained something to me about the possible time and the duration of the punishment, for it is difficult to conceive that a spirit could be somehow inserted into time.

> *In purgatory time is not as you perceive it on earth. But the souls do carry out various acts that succeed each other in the order of love; and this succession of continuous acts constitutes in a certain way the measure of a uniform time as you know it.*
>
> *Do not forget that a thousand years are as a single day in the eyes of the Almighty.*[8]

I saw that what constitutes the different grades of purgatory is not the nature of the punishment but its duration and intensity, whether greater or less, and at the same time a greater or lesser abundance of consolations. In spite of this, I saw that in the great purgatory (or the deepest purgatory), the demons are perceptible to souls, and this torments them greatly, because a great agitation reigns around them. This surprised me, but the angel explained it to me.

---

[8] Psalm 90:4.

The demons do not exercise a direct action on the souls in purgatory; they have no power over them. But the ability to notice their presence and their evil agitation is a torment permitted by God for certain souls.

The demon keeps what seems to be a residue of power, but these are only the aftereffects of sin.[9]

This kind of punishment endured by the souls in the great purgatory is nothing more than a moral irritation, a humiliation that increases their pain; their languishing of love is similar to the fire of purgatory. The stages differ in ways that are as distinct as this languishing of love can be, but in the last purification in the antechamber of heaven, this languishing no longer has different forms but exists alone.

The souls in purgatory suffer greatly from being forgotten by people on earth. They don't suffer for themselves, because there they no longer contemplate themselves.

---

[9] For St. Thomas Aquinas, the demons no longer have any power over the souls in purgatory. They can't torment them, because they have been definitively defeated. It is possible, writes St. Thomas, that the demons are present at the moment of death, when the soul separates from the body, seeing that they no longer have any rights over the soul, and also to see the soul suffer, thus satiating their hatred (*Summa Theologica*, q. 70 ter., a. 5).

St. Catherine of Siena and St. Bridget think instead that the demons are given the task of tormenting the souls in purgatory. The former writes of our Lord, saying: "I, the Eternal Truth, have made the demons my instruments to exercise my servants in virtue; at the same time as my avengers in regard to those who are suffering punishment in purgatory. Through them I show my justice to those who are condemned and to those who, in contrast to them, are souls in purgatory (J. Joubert and L. Cristiani, *Les plus beaux textes sur l'au-Delà*, [Paris: La Colombe, 1950], 27).

They suffer because they see a lack of attention and consideration for the communion of saints and for the glory of God, whom they love above all. They suffer the consequences of not receiving this great intercession that would shorten their expiatory sufferings. The souls who are suffering there don't want to leave purgatory for their own welfare, but for the greater glory of God, who is the only object of their loving gaze. These blessed souls can teach us a great deal about the mystery of the glory of God, our duty to glorify him, and our obligation to simplify our interior vision.

Absolutely everything for these souls—whether punishment or consolation—is a function of the glorification of God, their one and only occupation. They would gladly stay for a thousand years in purgatory if they could in this way increase the glory of God. Although they are not concerned about us, this does not mean that they don't love us! They love us a lot—more than any person here below, except perhaps some great saint. But they love us with the purest love of God. Their love is elevated and objective. When they pray for us, they only want our good, which is always ordered to the glory of God.

THE HOLINESS OF GOD

At the end of this morning's prayer, I received a teaching on the holiness of God; it was overpowering. I saw an immense sea of burning crystal, very peaceful and of an unfathomable depth. This sea communicated with the Holy Church, bathing it, permeating it, giving it food, and enlivening it. Every sin and imperfection was consumed in it, burning, erasing, and destroying in its fire every trace of impurity. All of heaven is submerged in this sea of crystal, illuminated and consumed by it. In it the Holy Church lives and subsists, constantly illuminated and purified by its ardor. In it also—in a mysterious way—the infernal abyss is contained.

I saw purgatory as the fiery antechamber of the celestial glory, where souls are submerged in the holiness of God in order to be purified. From this holiness of God, the souls in purgatory receive their greatest joy: their confirmation in grace and the certainty of their salvation; the impossibility of being able to sin any more and the joy in making expiation for God's glory. They rejoice also in being surrendered entirely in God's love. I saw that the slightest sin is an infinite offense to God, like an arrow launched at this sea of burning crystal. However, this arrow is lost and disappears, for this sea is immutable, unchanging, infinite. All this is incomprehensible to our spirit.[10]

I also saw the waves of the holiness of God pouring fully upon the innermost depths of purgatory: the souls there were permeated by it, submerging themselves in

---

[10] "And lo, a throne stood in heaven, with one seated on the throne! . . . and before the throne there is as it were a sea of glass, like crystal" (Revelation 4:2–6). The divine holiness is a mystery of the transcendence of God, the Beyond, who is fully self-sufficient and on whom all realities depend. Holiness is also in God the unfathomable perfection of his life of love. This life of love is communicated to man by the gift of grace. The sinner, preferring himself to God, offends the divine holiness. God is offended as the ultimate End, Doer of Good, Sovereign, Teacher, and Judge. Certainly the offense doesn't reach God in himself, but nevertheless it constitutes a grave injury to the consideration of the Creator, who is no longer glorified in man by a loving and grateful action.

it—although with terrible sufferings and hardship. The more they surrender themselves to this divine fire, in a violent impetus of love, the more they are transformed and become transparent, luminous, and beautiful—but also, at the same time, the more they suffer at seeing themselves in this sea and the more they want to remain there until they are totally purified. It is very difficult to translate these elevated intellectual visions.

The most surprising realization is that the holy souls in purgatory do not have any self-gaze or self-complacency; instead they are totally surrendered to divine Love. In their greatest sufferings they only have one desire: the glorification of God, and they are submerged in his holiness.

THE RIVER OF MERCY THAT SPRINGS FROM THE CROSS

Today our Lord gave me new lights about the mystery of purgatory. He showed me something like a river of abundant waters, springing from the cross at the death of the Savior: a merciful river of waters of fire.

I saw that purgatory was created by Christ the Savior—or more precisely, by the Father in him—when he died on the cross to save all mankind. He became the victor over death, whose empire was destroyed by him. Before the redemption of the human race by Christ's sacrifice, heaven was closed to us. Original sin had closed its gates, although divine love continued to attract the just. But it was necessary that Jesus Christ be made the gate of heaven by his death on the cross and his resurrection. Only he had the power to open what had been closed by man's sin. Only in him do we have access to heaven.[11]

Before the Redemption, just souls did not have access to heaven; they waited in limbo (the underworld). Divine love attracted them, but justice kept them separated from heaven. The gate had to be opened; it was opened by the crucified and glorified Savior. Now justice could exercise itself fully and be satisfied, and mercy, until then retained in God, could pour itself out fully on the human race. The Savior, who is merciful love, united infinite love and strict justice by his passion and death.[12]

Christ the Redeemer gave us purgatory as a pledge—a place of strict justice and infinite love where souls dedicated to the infinite love of God can nevertheless, if necessary, pay their debt to divine justice.[13]

I hope you will forgive my poor ability to express myself, but if what I write is obscure and confusing, my mother the Church will be able to explain it. In that interior light, I saw purgatory as a river of fire, a river of mercy springing from the Cross. In this river of mercy, souls are invested with the burning love of God who wants to purify

---

[11] Our Lady is greeted in Tradition as "*Janua Coeli*," Gate of Heaven (see The Litany of Loreto), because, having been given to us by Christ the Savior, she is united to him in the work of salvation: she leads us to Jesus, who is not only the gate of heaven, but heaven itself. And in the measure in which Mary enables us to reach Jesus, she is, with him, the gate of heaven.

[12] "The Paschal Mystery is the culmination of this revealing and effecting of mercy, which is able to justify man, to restore justice in the sense of that salvific order which God willed from the beginning in man and, through man, in the world" (John Paul II, *Dives in Misericordia*, no. 7).

[13] In purgatory, justice and mercy fuse together, but purgatory reveals divine mercy more. "Some theologians affirm that mercy is the greatest of the attributes and perfections of God" (*Dives in Misericordia*, no. 13).

them and introduce them into his eternal intimacy in heaven. I saw that heaven is attainable to us in Christ, who is the ever-open door, but to pass through this door one has to have fulfilled every debt to divine justice.

Purgatory is precisely the place where souls pay these debts. I saw it as a river of fire fed by the flames of divine mercy, and these flames spring from the heart of Christ, pierced on the cross for the salvation of the human race. In this sense, purgatory is in the merciful heart of Jesus, and so is the Church militant. All is summed up in love.

THE SEAL OF THE CROSS IS UPON PURGATORY

While I was praying the Rosary for the poor and blessed souls of purgatory, I saw purgatory as a highly populated place, situated in the center of the earth. To me this was a symbol to help us understand that the souls in purgatory are very far from the glory of heaven and very much separated from us. A large, dark red cross appeared to be perched above purgatory, guarding its limits and separating it on the one hand from heaven and on the other from earth. I saw that our prayers and suffrages go first to heaven, where they are then distributed in a rain of consolation on purgatory. The same thing happens with the prayers, requests, and graces the saints obtain for purgatory. They rain down on them in the same way: by virtue of the cross. My guardian angel then appeared to me.

The seal of the cross is placed above purgatory. The holy cross is the sign of mercy and the instrument of your salvation. By it you are given all the necessary graces for your sanctification. Purgatory is a

*gift of merciful love and salvation springing from
the holy cross. For this reason the cross is located
over purgatory, as it is placed above everything that
is ordained to your salvation.*

After speaking, he indicated by a sign that I should continue praying for the souls in purgatory. I finished praying
the Rosary. Then the angel continued:

*Without the cross, there would be no Church,
nor any purgatory either. The holy Church is the
Church of Jesus crucified; one should enter with
him into the mystery of the cross to arrive with him
to the light of eternal glory.*

    *Purgatory allows numerous souls who have
not fully entered into Jesus crucified, who have not
taken up in themselves the vocation of victim, to be
"finished off" in Jesus crucified, and thus go with
him to the glory of heaven.*

    The cross is placed over purgatory like a seal . . .

GOD LOVES THE SOULS IN PURGATORY

On this day especially consecrated to the souls of the
departed, my guardian angel appeared to my interior
vision and told me:

Look and give thanks to the All Powerful!

I saw purgatory totally submerged in a triple ray of
light, water, and blood coming forth from the Eucharistic
Heart of Jesus. My soul was jubilant before that splendid
vision, and the angel continued:

*This is so that you understand how much God loves
these blessed souls, for they are holy, as you know. In
the river of blood that bathes purgatory, the Father
contemplates with mercy the souls who are suffering.
He sees them redeemed by the blood of his divine
Son and finds his greatest glory in their salvation.*

*In this river of clear water poured like a refresh-
ing cloud on purgatory, submerging the souls in it
and cleansing them, Jesus invites them to enter into
the glory of heaven, and he attracts them in himself
to the Father.*

*In this river of burning light that illuminates
the mystery of purgatory, the Spirit pours forth
his flames of love through the Eucharistic Heart of
Jesus to engulf the holy souls.*

I was filled with joy on hearing these words. The angel
concluded:

*The Blessed Trinity loves the souls in purgatory.
The Father loves them in his Son, and in their common Spirit, the Son loves them through the Father.*

*The Spirit loves them with the Father and the
Son; each of the three Divine Persons contemplates
in these souls the great mystery of man's salvation,
which is their greatest glory and the motive behind
their constant rejoicing.*

*The Father has saved men through the Son, the
Son has redeemed them through the Father, and
the Spirit carries out in them the salvation that the
Father proposes to them in the Son. Their glory is
perfect, and their rejoicing is perfect.*

These words were not easy for me to understand, but the angel invited me to write them just as he had dictated them. I hope that I have not made any mistakes. *Deo Gratias!* Everything then disappeared from my interior vision.

THE DAWNING OF ETERNAL DAY

"And night shall be no more; they need no light of lamp or sun, for the Lord God will be their light, and they shall reign for ever and ever" (Revelation 22:5).

This is the splendid vision of heaven given us by the Lord in the Book of Revelation. Every day I read and meditated on a passage of Scripture, and these words of the apostle John have helped me very much. I was meditating on this verse to sustain my faith and nourish my hope, when suddenly my soul felt a strong inclination to pray for the souls in purgatory and ask for their liberation, so that they might savor in heaven this gentle light of God.

I understood that purgatory is a zone of twilight in relation to the light of paradise and related to faith here below on earth. This was not a vision, nor an image, but the fruit of prayer abandoned to the inspiration of the Holy Spirit.

It seemed to me that on earth it is nighttime, and we work to attain the eternal day of heaven. We receive lights and consolations in great number, thanks to the Church that teaches us, nourishes us, and helps us . . . All of this should help us to reach heaven. If we have completed our work in a satisfactory way and on time, we will enter heaven to receive our recompense and our repose. If our work was not done well because we have done it carelessly or not taken advantage of or despised and profaned the helps we have received, there is condemnation and eternal night. . . . May the Lord preserve us from that!

If our work is not finished, we have to go to purgatory, into this dawn that precedes the day, the zone of shadow before the light of heaven. But there the souls cannot work anymore: in purgatory one cannot acquire merit. We have to wait there until our brothers on earth, with their prayers and suffrages, complete our unfinished work and rectify it, since the work of humanity all contributes to the glory of God for the building up of his kingdom.

THE FIERY ANTECHAMBER TO THE HOUSE OF HEAVEN

I was given a very clear interior vision showing purgatory as a fiery antechamber (or waiting room) in the house of the Father where certain souls have to spend a certain amount of time before entering the heavenly dwelling place. At the same time I saw a very beautiful image.

I saw heaven as a large house, with a combination of impressive buildings joined to one another by galleries of light and surrounded by a splendid garden. This garden was fenced by a wall of light and guarded by hundreds of angels. In the middle of the garden was a magnificent tree with green leaves. It was loaded with a great variety of exquisite fruits and garlands of perfumed flowers. It was a symbolic representation of the tree of the cross and the graces that flow from it. A resplendent sun poured its light everywhere, resembling a fountain of light with seven sources.

I saw thousands of souls arriving at the gates of heaven. Some were invited into the mansions of the Father; others, more numerous, were conducted by the angels to the vestibule of fire in these heavenly mansions. These souls needed to be purified there of the spots and shadows that stained their white robes, the remains of old cleansed blotches that had not yet totally disappeared.

In heaven, some angels and saints gathered all kinds and varieties of fruit and flowers from the tree of the cross, depositing them in beautiful golden baskets that other angels carried to the Church on earth to give to the souls on earth and also to the vestibule of fire to help the souls that were in purgatory. From earth thousands of angels returned to heaven with baskets filled with grains of incense that burned before the face of God, incense made up of the good works and prayers of the Church here below. A certain quantity of these grains were burned on different altars where angels gathered fruit and sometimes flowers that were destined for the vestibule of fire.

I understood that the incense represented the suffrages for the poor and holy souls in purgatory. All of this activity was done in an environment of happy and joyful light. . . . I also saw that the more suffrages and prayers, the more numerous the fruit and flowers—fruit and flowers symbolizing the graces that console the souls and shorten their time of purification and ease their torments. Souls arrive unceasingly in the vestibule of fire (purgatory) to enter into heaven illuminated with whiteness. They are united to the multitude of the saints singing the praises of God, united to him forever and exultant with joy.

A PRISONER OF MERCY GUARDED BY JUSTICE

In numerous interior visions that our Lord granted to me in regard to purgatory, I was able to penetrate somewhat into this great mystery, which I judge to have been necessary for my unworthiness and for the personal edification of those who read these pages. Undoubtedly he thought of sanctifying others by confiding the secrets of his heart to an instrument of so little value. . . . In reading these pages he allows people to pray for me.

I have seen purgatory as a mystical prison, raised by divine mercy[14] and guarded by justice, but this jail has certain peculiarities that make it a unique place. Purgatory can be described as a prison of light and fire, constructed by divine mercy; the soul needs to be cleansed there of the punishment due to its sin in order to be able to enter into eternal happiness—it has to be cleansed of all that still delays its entry. But the most notable thing about this prison is that it does not have any walls or

---

[14] How does purgatory show divine mercy? Given that it prepares souls for the vision of glory, purgatory recalls the merciful offering that Jesus made on the cross for the purpose of opening heaven to mankind. Without the cross, there would be no purgatory because there would be no heaven either. This is precisely why purgatory is directed to a great number of souls.

In addition, as a state of purification, purgatory also appears as a marvelous gift of the wounded heart of the immolated Lamb, who brings the possibility of a final purification to souls, if at the end of their earthly life they are not prepared for the encounter with the living and true God. Without this possibility, the soul could not attain its end; this would be hell. God satisfies his justice in purgatory, but in the very exercise of his justice lives mercy, which connects man in a special way to the restoration of the rights of love, which has been mocked by sin.

cells, nor does it have guards; the soul freely guards itself with no more coercion that its total conformity to the pure will of God. The soul is not closed in; it remains by itself in purgatory freely. Having a clear vision of itself and the incapacity to enter into heaven, it allows itself to be held and attracted by the divine love that invites it and holds it in its expiation so it can become worthy—no matter how much it costs—of the demands of divine mercy that it has to satisfy.

The only gate of this mystical prison is divine justice; the only condition required of the soul is giving itself lovingly to God, who attracts it powerfully with his impulses of love and demands of justice. The soul burns with the desire of throwing itself into the infinite love, but it cannot do this as long as it has not satisfied its duties toward divine justice. This is purgatory.

I have seen that a soul would prefer a thousand times more to remain in purgatory until the final judgment rather than risk (if that were possible) entering into God's intimacy without having paid the totality of its debt to divine justice. It prefers to be purified and have its clothes washed again and again before arriving at God's banquet with some shadow of a blemish. But in fact, this is not something that souls in purgatory request, because they see the mercy with such clarity that they give themselves over to God entirely, letting him direct their purification and their liberation.

A vision of the great purgatory[15]

When I had finished getting ready for bed and was praying for the souls in purgatory, my angel appeared and told me very seriously:

Look, my child, and pray a lot!

I saw with the eyes of my soul a frightful fire without limit or form that burned without ever changing in an overwhelming silence. There was no sound, not the slightest outburst; the fire appeared to be immobile, always burning with the same intensity and with an unmatched violence. My whole body felt this fire, and I experienced a terrible thirst. This terrified me. My fear increased when I saw that, in the midst of this fire, thousands and thousands of poor souls pressed against one another, but without any communication between them other than that of the fire itself. They appeared to be pressed down—one might say crushed—by the very fire in which they found themselves. What I was contemplating was the great purgatory, which, if I understood it rightly, is equal to hell except in the duration of the suffering and the hatred for God and other souls; neither was there any hopelessness there. This terrifying state cannot be adequately explained, but this is how I perceived it.

---

[15] There is only one purgatory. The Church has never made a pronouncement about this triple aspect: the great purgatory, median (or middle) purgatory, and the antechamber of heaven. But by analogy with spiritual progress (conversion, advancement, and perfection), described well by St. Paul (see Philippians 3:12–14), it is considered useful to contemplate the purification in its three successive phases. The whole work of St. John of the Cross, which likens purification and purgatory, is an illustration of this subject.

The souls in this great purgatory are submerged in an arid and dry hope, bound and enclosed in the fire of divine love by a great loneliness, and locked in a sorrowful but serene face-to-face encounter with the divine will. It seemed to me that all these souls were looking toward God, but in a confused way—that is, without perceiving him in a precise manner but simply turned toward him in a very painful way. If I am not mistaken, I saw that, in this state, they are more purified than consoled, more burned than illumined. It is a terrible state.

I was able to understand that the most important thing for the souls who are there is the long work of permanent destruction of the "crust"[16]—that is, the penalty of sin. This is somehow a passive purification, although the soul cooperates with all its strength in the perfect union of its whole being with the will of God. But thanks to God's love, in this state the soul cannot measure its purification nor perceive the progressive work of this purification that is occurring within it. The soul does not feel the slightest progress or the slightest improvement in its torment. The souls there don't know how long their torment will last. They only know—because they have a sufficiently precise knowledge of this—that they are saved. It is as though they are submerged in a mystery of profound solitude, but in spite of that, they know they have not been abandoned by God or the Church. Their knowledge is, however, so vague and so general that they feel their situation cruelly, and they have no other consolation than this very dry

---

[16] In regard to this question, see the section entitled "The state of the souls in purgatory."

hope. Their powers are mysteriously incapable of anything but a blind submission to the demands of God's holiness.[17]

This state of the great purgatory is very painful, but there are some consolations. The first and most important is simply the knowledge of being saved, with a total and pacifying certainty, as well as a source of consolation, peace, joy, gratitude toward God, and a desire for his glorification. There are also certain sparks and flashes, as you would see in a blacksmith's shop. It is a fire that looks almost black as it burns. At least that's how it appeared to me. Our Lord perhaps wanted me to understand in a symbolic way the purifying effect on the souls there. In that purifying fire there are distant lights and deaf echoes of the joy of heaven and the prayers of the Church for the souls in purgatory. But in this great purgatory, the souls do not feel the goodness or consolation that suffrages in their favor are procuring for them. On the other hand, their worst torment is their desire for God, which is enlivened at every moment; they suffer since they are not able to perceive how God is lovingly answering them.

These poor souls in the great purgatory are not able to enjoy other, sweeter consolations that souls in median

---

[17] "One has to always remember about the infallible precision of divine justice, always accompanied by his mercy. Justice demands that the punishments of purgatory be set according to the faults that have to be purified. It can happen that, having lived a life of crime, a man makes at the last moment such acts of faith and of love, that in an instant he expiates for all of his faults, as was the case of the good thief to whom Our Lord said: 'Today you will be with me in paradise.' And the contrary may happen: that having avoided hell very narrowly, a long expiation may be imposed before entering heaven. Between the greatest and least culpability there is a scale of values that we cannot even imagine" (Father Monsabrè, cited by J. Joubert and L. Cristiani, *Les plus beaux textes*, 220).

purgatory, and especially those in the antechamber to heaven, enjoy. They do not have the happiness of seeing the Virgin Mary and the saints who are praying for them in heaven, nor do they generally see their guardian angels who pray for them unceasingly. On certain liturgical feasts, they hear and see something of the feasts and joys of heaven, and this encourages and consoles them. As far as the suffrages that the Church militant applies for them, these souls do not perceive them, but these suffrages have the effect of shortening their time in the great purgatory.

While I contemplated this mystery, I prayed with fervor for these suffering souls, and I asked my guardian angel to join me in this. How was it possible to bear such suffering and torment? My angel took me firmly by the arm, surely to help me understand that he was assisting me and communicating the grace of contemplating these supernatural realities. He himself then said to me with great seriousness:

You know that the slightest fault is an infinite offense against God.[18] These blessed souls also know this, and they do not cease, in the midst of their sufferings, to thank the All Powerful for the

---

[18] "Dost thou not know, my daughter, that all the sufferings which the soul endures, or can endure, in this life, are insufficient to punish one smallest fault because the offense being done to me, who am the infinite Good, calls for an infinite satisfaction? However, I wish that thou shouldst know that not all the pains that are given to men in this life are given as punishments, but as corrections, in order to chastise my children when they offend; although it is true that both the guilt and the penalty can be expiated by the desire of the soul, that is by true contrition, not through the pain endured but through an infinite desire; because God, who is infinite love wishes an infinite sorrow" (St. Catherine of Siena, *Dialogues*, ch. III [Rockford, Ill.: TAN Books, 1974], 30.).

*lightness of their sentences—since the punishment
is finite while the offense is infinite, and because
often there has been more than one offense but
many infinite offenses.*

*In the great purgatory there are souls of great
sinners, but there are many more souls who
received many graces and did not respond to them,
souls that had to accept weighty responsibilities
and did not know how to take them on perfectly.
Therefore, in the great purgatory you will see a
large number of consecrated souls and priests,
prelates, bishops, cardinals, and popes. You will
also see many political governors, chiefs of state
and leaders of the people, kings, emperors, princes,
and governors.*

*All these poor souls have to endure the pains
of the great purgatory together with criminals,
libertines, and all the great sinners saved by divine
mercy who were able—sometimes at the last
moment—to escape the eternal abyss . . .*

*Pray, pray a lot, and get others to pray for these
souls! Pray also very especially for the consecrated
and for your directors, because they have a special
accounting to render to God.*

Remain in peace and be faithful!

When he was finished with this teaching, the vision of
the great purgatory closed, while voices sang with a tone
of great sadness: "My soul thirsts for God, for the living
God. When shall I come and behold the face of God?"[19]

---

[19] Psalm 42:3.

Then all of this disappeared from my interior view. During this vision, my skin had reddened, and I burned as though I had exposed myself to the sun too much; my cracked lips and hands hurt me. *Thanks be to God!* Our Lord at times permits some exterior signs to dissipate any doubts I might have. Although these signs are annoying and at times painful, they are no more than a small offering for these blessed souls in purgatory—their value at best amounts to no more than that.

A VISION OF MIDDLE PURGATORY

At night, when I, in silence and solitude, prayed a little for the souls in purgatory, my guardian angel appeared to me, surrounded by light. Stretching forth his hand, he said to me:

Look, my child, and pray a lot!

I saw once more with the eyes of my soul a sea of fire burning before me with a great roar. Immense flames came and went without stopping, sizzling and hissing so loudly it was deafening. In the midst of this, thousands of souls extended their hands, whipped by this fire that lifted them up with a kind of impetuous blowing. This spectacle made me retreat and pray still more earnestly, but at the same time it seemed to me that I was in this fire myself, buffeted by flames that struck me untiringly. My mouth became very dry, and I felt faint, as though I were suffocating.

It seemed to me that all the souls that I saw were suffering this torture themselves; they were suffocating and not static as was the case yesterday. In this vision I perceived a movement that seemed quiet and violent at the same time, almost insensible in its manifestations and nevertheless dynamic. The souls in this movement appeared to have a confused and very painful perception of it. In this part of purgatory, there is a movement of the soul toward heaven, yet without the least personal desire; it is an interior impetus that pushes them, as if God was inclining toward them to draw them to himself. All of this is difficult to express.

From the beginning of this contemplation, I understood that this was the median, or middle, purgatory, where souls see themselves in the midst of a clear fire. They are alone in the presence of the sanctity and majesty of God, in an unspeakable hope that is their consolation. They are allowed to perceive God in his mercy, and they never cease to glorify him. They have more precise knowledge of God than the souls in the great purgatory; they are purified by what they suffer, but they are also enlightened, which consoles them and allows them to give glory to God. They not only surrender themselves to the divine will, they express their gratitude. It is a state of great suffering and great consolation.

In the great purgatory, souls are passively surrendered to the will of God in an arid hope; here, in middle purgatory, they are attracted to God and see him clearly, but they cannot approach him. They are both drawn to God and yet held firmly back. But they are totally submissive to divine love, accepting with gratitude the fire, the sufferings, and the tearing apart without being in the least concerned with its duration or the intensity of these pains. They suffer without knowing anything more. They do not look at themselves, and they do not have the capacity, the will, or the desire to ask anything. They love, pray, and expiate for love in a loving availability to the holiness of God.

The souls in middle purgatory suffer quite a lot. I think these souls feel even more attracted to God as they approach the end of their time in purgatory. An ardent desire for God grows in them, and they also grow more in suffering: The closer one comes to the goal, the more desire one has to arrive there. It is the same way in purgatory, but God does not let the soul know the hour of liberation; the loving suffering only grows, while the pains of the senses progressively disappear. In middle purgatory the souls enjoy consolations and joys that, in addition to filling them with joy and gratitude, inflame them with the desire to see God, and this increases that great suffering of *not* seeing him.

The first consolation they have is the ability to perceive the infinite tenderness of God toward them. They perceive the impulse of love that attracts them, and they feel this with the deepest joy and suffering—and with this their love increases. From time to time, they are shown the suffrages being applied to them, the prayers and good works arising from earth to the throne of the Trinity destined for them. This fills them with happiness, and they give thanks. But, on the other hand, they can also see those who have forgotten them completely and do not pray for them. This fills them with sadness, not for themselves but for those persons who are thus deprived of graces, and above all because they see how little the glory of God is served, adored, and loved. This causes them great pain.

Another consolation for the souls in middle purgatory is receiving frequent visits from the Mother of God. She comes to comfort them, help them, and reassure them that she is their gentle Mother and the messenger of divine love. The Virgin Mary goes to purgatory on all her feasts, and each time she releases a great number of souls. The souls in the great purgatory do not have the consolation of seeing her, while the souls in middle purgatory benefit from these regular visits. They also have the joy of frequently seeing their guardian angels and their patron saints, who pray for them, exhort them to have patience and peace, and stimulate them to love and gratitude.

I was taught also that the blessed souls in middle purgatory receive permission at times from Our Lord to reveal themselves to us here below, whether this is to show us the mystery of purgatory, or call us to prayer, or even warn us of some of the dangers shown to them by the mercy of God. I have seen very clearly that these manifestations—which are poorly known and sometimes called phantasms—are frequently visits from the souls in purgatory. Frequently, but not always: Satan is the father of lies, the master of illusion and fraud. Those simulated apparitions shown in sessions of spiritism are never souls in purgatory. They are diabolical spirits that take the name and even at times the appearance of known persons in order to lie, tempt, falsify people's judgment, etc. Spiritism is a work of hell, a true satanic religion based on vanity, curiosity, and deceit. It is raging right now.

My guardian angel, who is at my side, comforts me and enlightens me by saying gently:

You can see middle purgatory; it is a less terrible state than the great purgatory.

But you should not think that this is a matter of two grades or two independent states: in general all the souls who have to suffer these punishments pass through the great purgatory before entering middle purgatory. It is very rare that a soul does not go through the great purgatory. Souls stay there for a longer or shorter time—at times for only a minute, at other times for years, and still other times for centuries. Sin is an infinite offense to God. . . . Often, from the particular judgment, the soul goes to the great purgatory. It is there as brutish, crushed, for it has discovered sin in its gravity, its effects, and its implications. In view of this, the soul is paralyzed: it contemplates both the justice of God that is acting on it and the mercy of God that has granted it salvation. Afterward it starts to move toward God, who attracts it and teaches it through the support of his infinite love, and that is when the soul enters middle purgatory.

In middle purgatory the soul remains facing love. It contemplates this infinite love that attracts it; it sees it poured over it in plenitude, certainly, but also over the entire Church. In middle purgatory, the soul comes out of itself and discovers all it means to belong to the Church. You will see in middle purgatory souls of every kind, ages, and times. You must pray for them without ceasing. You must pray for all the souls in purgatory!

Then the vision of purgatory disappeared from my interior sight, and in the distance I heard voices singing: "Lord, all my longing is known to thee, my sighing is not hidden from thee. . . ."[20]

A VISION OF THE ANTECHAMBER OF HEAVEN

Next the angel showed me the antechamber of heaven, which could be described as the summit of purgatory, it is a world of searing light and peace. It appeared to be an extension of very pale fire with an enormous intensity and profundity; it was immersed in the light that shines forth from heaven. There I saw thousands and thousands of souls in prayer, in peace, submerged in an unheard of fire of love and suffering. My soul became submerged in this fire that seemed to pass through my veins like great burning waves. My whole body was burning, but a sweet calmness at the same time invaded my soul, and I prayed in silence.

One cannot really explain what the antechamber of heaven is like: it is a suffering of love carried to its paradoxical maximum: a pure suffering of love and the greatest happiness, the most gentle united to the most terrible suffering. But I cannot say any more than this. The souls in the antechamber of heaven are attracted with an ineffable encouragement by love that saturates them and communicates itself to them with superabundance; they respond

---

[20] Psalm 38:9.

with ardor, surrendering themselves totally to this desire for divine love that makes them happy and captivates them even though they cannot yet attain it. It is the summit of love they experience, a pure suffering of love.

In the antechamber of heaven, there is no pain other than this, but . . . what intensity! The souls in the antechamber have great and constant consolations, which are also a veritable torture of love. Love gives itself, and they want nothing more than to respond to it, but they are still not able to do this fully. Love gives everything, they receive everything, but they cannot attain it. How can this be explained?

These blessed souls are in a constant jubilation; they are happy. They glorify God and surrender themselves to his loving attraction, and they are in something like an agony of love because they cannot glorify him as they should—since they can only do this in heaven—and cannot unite themselves to him, who calls, attracts, and awaits them in a yearning of extraordinary love.

There is nothing more in the antechamber—there is no other punishment; all the suffering has passed (if one can express it this way). In love, the soul becomes unified: Suffering and love are united in a complete simplification when the last atom of suffering, yearning, and desire has been consumed by love and absorbed by it, and the door to heaven opens.

But these blessed souls do not know when that will happen. They have no perception and cannot evaluate the intensity of what they are enduring. They experience both pain and love in their suffering—I don't know how to adequately explain it. They surrender to the flame of love that burns them, illuminates them, and makes them agonize out of desire for love. They perceive the love of God, and receive love's gifts, caresses, and manifestations, but they do not have any other desire than to reach their common end, attain it, and then never abandon it.

The antechamber is a foretaste of heaven, and therefore it is given this name, but there is in this foretaste as much suffering as love—and *what* suffering! In heaven there is no longer any suffering nor shadow of pain, but here it seems that all the suffering, all the punishment has been concentrated and united into a sole service of love. I would like to find fitting words to express this, but my vocabulary is insufficient to translate what I do not know; even in the most sublime ecstasies and raptures, it could not be known other than in an approximate and temporary way.

In the antechamber the souls enjoy great consolations that stimulate their desire for love. They contemplate their guardian angels, who are continually at their side, inciting them to an incessant joy and thanksgiving. They are favored by visits of the saints, especially their holy patrons and St. Joseph, the archangel St. Michael, who is the great angel of purgatory, and above all, the Virgin Mary, who very frequently (especially on the days of her liturgical feasts and every Saturday) consoles these blessed souls, bringing them the happiness of heaven, hope, and waves of divine love. These souls marvel and are filled with gratitude, love, and yearning, and they are so close to participating in the heavenly liturgies, harmonies, and splendors that they perceive at every moment, which enlivens even more their sorrow of love and their desire for God.

It seems to me that they have all there is in heaven *except* the vision and possession of God, and this absence is what causes them such terrible suffering. For only the vision and possession of the supreme good can calm their souls; although they receive the most sublime gifts, they continue to yearn for love because they do not yet have infinite love.

The souls in the antechamber of heaven are very enlightened about the needs of the Church militant, and they pray to God for our intentions. We frequently forget that the souls in purgatory pray for us and think of us much more than we think of them. They ask the greatest good for us—that is, the greater glory of God—and they have a great solicitude for us. They also receive at times, according to the needs of the Church or of a particular soul, the very special mission of showing themselves to us—to warn us, exhort us, or simply to draw our attention to the mystery of purgatory and ask for our prayers and good works.

I have said everything I can say about this, although what I was able to see is infinitely clearer and superior to what I am capable of expressing. My soul was immersed in this gentle and painful contemplation. Then the angel told me:

> *You have contemplated the antechamber of heaven.*
> *It is a kingdom of pure love and pure suffering:*
> *the souls advance toward the heavenly Jerusalem;*
> *they arrive before their King. There they remain*
> *for a greater or lesser time, but never as long as in*
> *the great purgatory or middle purgatory, for the*

intensity of their yearning for love in the ante-chamber of heaven constitutes a rapid and final purification.

You have to pray much for these blessed souls— above all offer your Communions for them. This powerfully help bring about their liberation.

Then the antechamber was erased from my interior vision. While I remained in an act of thanksgiving, I saw the souls singing in a gentle way: "For thou hast delivered my soul from death, yea, my feet from falling, that I may walk before God in the light of life."[21]

A VISION OF HOPE AND PEACE

The Feast of St. Paschal Baylon, the saint of the Holy Eucharist. During Mass I asked St. Paschal's intercession for those consecrated persons in purgatory who are awaiting the help and the consolations of our prayers. During the act of thanksgiving I prayed the Stations of the Cross for that intention. At the end of this prayer, our Lord showed me an interior vision with impressive images of great impact. I saw the rain of souls that I mentioned previously. The greater part were going to purgatory in a serene silence. At the same time I saw thousands and thousands of souls being raised from purgatory like brilliant stars and entering into the glory of paradise, escorted by a light. During this entire vision, there was an incessant movement of souls, the light fall of snowflakes toward purgatory, the flaming ascension of souls attaining

---

[21] Psalm 56:13.

the conquest of heaven who were like brilliant stars. All of this was like an extraordinary ballet, a splendor of light, love, and grace.

I don't think that it would be disrespectful to compare purgatory to a hive of gold situated in the garden of God and animated by an incessant oscillation. A hive of expiation in which the bees gather in the flowerbeds of mercy, or a hive of prayer where they make the honey of their celestial glory (thanks to the prayer of the Church and its intentions), and from whence they undertake their flight toward heaven forever. I was shown that in the bosom of purgatory there are always a number of souls who are very superior to people still on earth, and masses and masses arrive each day. Others leave to wash themselves in the splendors of heaven. There are far more souls in purgatory than in hell, although this also, unfortunately, is too greatly populated. One can have no idea of the great number of souls who are lost, and if the certainty that there are more chosen than condemned has to console us and move us to give thanks to God, it should not, however, make us forget that hell exists. If we knew this, we would radically change our lives. My holy guardian angel revealed various things to me that I will note here because of their instructive value:

> Too many souls are in the abyss of the eternal inferno. The danger of being condemned is always growing due to the aberrations of your way of living, which you mistakenly call—with as much blindness as vanity—the progress of civilization.
>
> Is it progress that this society gives more importance to what is passing, to ephemeral and deceitful

*satisfactions, than to the eternal truths and the life
of the soul in God? There is not one soul out of ten
that is working for its salvation.*

The angel continued very seriously with another subject that he spoke about very rarely, undoubtedly because of its prophetic aspect.

*You are entering a very serious period: Because of
the attacks perpetrated directly against life and
against the very fountains of life, God is ready to
punish humanity in the measure of its tremendous
crimes. You are facing the rigors of divine justice!*

He then showed me a shower of souls which were elevated to a very gentle clarity; I understood that those were the hundreds and thousands of children assassinated in the wombs of their mothers. Those little ones were not going to heaven but to what is traditionally called limbo. Limbo is a heaven without the glory of the beatific vision of God, or a hell without any suffering—I don't quite know how to explain it. There is there a kind of happiness there, but it is not the celestial blessedness. This is where the little ones go who have not lived outside of their mothers, as well as the little children who have died without receiving baptism.

Limbo can be described as the heaven of innocence, where all those little souls enjoy a limited happiness. I believe that, at the end of time, limbo will be recapitulated in heaven, but I don't know how. All those little ones sing the glory of God for being alive and participating in life, which is a gift of God.

This vision of limbo was a little bit sad for my soul.[22] After this, the angel said before disappearing:

The holiness of God makes great demands upon you. You very frequently forget that you are created in the image and likeness of God! You also forget that you have been ransomed by the blood of Christ.

But the divine Trinity is going to raise up from among you an army of saints, a great number of adorers, who will despise the vain attractions of the world and consecrate themselves solely to the glorification of God. They will work in silence and adoration for the salvation of all their brethren.

Yes, divine mercy will touch many souls who will close their ears to the clamors of the world and will hear at last the calls to conversion that our

---

[22] The name "limbo of the patriarchs" or "the bosom of Abraham" is used for the place where the just of the Old Testament were before the coming of Christ and the realization of the salvation of mankind by the sacrifice of the cross. There the just did not suffer, but their rest was incomplete due to the absence of the beatific vision that was to be obtained for them by the sacrifice of Jesus. The mystery of the redemption made it possible for all the just to leave this place and enter into glory accompanying Jesus.

One should not confuse the bosom of Abraham with the "limbo" that, according to a tradition supported by common teaching, was where children who died without baptism went. But it is important to note that the *Catechism of the Catholic Church* makes no allusion to this tradition, being content to declare: "As regards children who have died without baptism, the Church can only entrust them to the mercy of God, as she does in her funeral rites for them. Indeed, the great mercy of God who desires that all men should be saved (see 1 Timothy 2:4), and Jesus's tenderness toward children which caused him to say: 'Let the children come to me, do not hinder them' (Mark 10:14), allow us to hope that there is a way of salvation for children who have died without baptism. All the more urgent is the Church's call not to prevent little children coming to Christ through the gift of holy baptism" (CCC, 1261).

*Lord never ceases to direct to them. And with the
sole desire of the glory of God, the blessed souls
in purgatory are working to obtain for you
this flourishing of holiness for the time that is
approaching. . . . You will understand this later.*

The angel then became silent and disappeared from my
interior vision, leaving me in peace and consolation. May
our prayers accelerate this flourishing of holiness!

THE STATE OF THE SOULS IN PURGATORY

During my afternoon prayer, while meditating on some
points of the Gospel, I suddenly saw my angel appear
before me in a vivid light. He said strongly: "Praised be
Jesus Christ!" I answered in the customary way, and he
continued:

*Our most Holy God wants to grant you today a
knowledge of the state of the souls who find themselves in purgatory so you will pray for them and
thus help them more effectively.*

He extended his hand toward a bright light, and I saw
with clarity something like diamonds covered by a dark
crust. A ray of fire struck this crust and progressively illuminated it, revealing the precious gems that gleamed with
all their splendor and purity. While I contemplated this,
the angel said:

*This image can help you understand the mystery
of the souls in purgatory. A soul that is in purgatory is static in its degree of holiness and love; it is*

confirmed in grace and is holy. Its charity will not grow any more—it is revealed in its plenitude, and it expands. For this reason you see the souls like perfect, pure, sparkling diamonds.[23]

In the particular judgment, the soul is detached from all sin and from all imperfection; there only remains the debt of their sin—that is to say, the punishment they have to undergo and expiate. That punishment is symbolized by the dark crust covering the diamond; the punishment does not affect the soul or injure it, but it is an obstacle and the cause of the expiatory sufferings. The punishment is above the soul, not in it, although the soul feels its effects.[24]

---

[23] In purgatory, the souls enjoy the security of reaching the glorious vision. They also have the certainty of not being able to sin. Because of this confirmation in grace, the Church has the custom of calling them "the holy souls in purgatory." We can add that they can no longer merit; their time of meriting is completed, and their charity will not grow any more. The degree of glory that one enjoys in heaven corresponds to the degree of charity they had at the moment of death. These truths, which have been recorded very succinctly, are presented with certainty by almost all theologians.

[24] According to a felicitous formulation of Cardinal Journet, "The penalty follows the sin like a shadow follows a body." The notion of penalty is complex. It is the price of sin; said in another way: "It is what the sin deserves." After death, in purgatory the soul expiates the temporal punishment it owes to divine justice. This punishment is constituted by the sufferings of purgatory: The soul accepts the debt of its sin with patience and love. But this acceptance is not yet, properly speaking, a satisfaction, for it is no longer meritorious. If the soul suffers the purification that frees it of its debt to God, it does not assume it spontaneously, as it would on earth by a meritorious act, which is satisfaction. Therefore, the soul does not merit now the lessening or attenuation of the punishment, but it obtains it when it is paid, or abbreviated by the "suffrages of the living" (see Garrigou-Lagrange, *Life Everlasting*, 276).

*The fire of divine love that strikes the soul con-
stitutes the punishment that produces the suffering
of expiation. This action of fire provides the weight
of the punishment, which constitutes the suffering
itself of purgatory.*

The soul discovers its own splendor; progressively,
with a continuous burning, the crust dissolves and disappears, and the diamond is little by little purified and elevated in all its perfection. In purgatory, a soul is a perfect
diamond that is covered by the crust of its penalty. Beneath
the action of divine fire, it is lessened continually until
finally it disappears completely. . . . The angel continued
his teaching:

*In purgatory the soul is conformed to perfect
charity and in submission to the divine will.
It is united in its free and total consent to the
desire of God's love for it. Its only desire is to
do the will of God; it has no other will than this
pure desire.*[25]
*The soul enters purgatory on its own, because
it is in some way being pushed by its love for God's
glory, holiness, and justice.*

The souls of purgatory know a certain kind of happiness by giving glory to God, situating this glory above their
own immediate interest, and they accept and even grasp
with joy and loving gratitude the expiation of their sins.
My angel then said:

---

[25] See St. Catherine of Genoa, *Treatise on Purgatory*, II, p. 30.

This joy is like a foretaste of eternal holiness. The souls in purgatory are not resigned but totally absorbed by God, and they are very active in the service of his name, his glorification—although this involves a great suffering for them. They have the surety that purgatory is not eternal and will permit them the definitive vision of God. In purgatory the suffering of the souls is also the cause of their happiness; their happiness is equally their punishment.[26]

One cannot understand this without marveling. These souls are saints. They are surrendered to the love of God; they are possessed by his love, to which they raise no resistance although the divine action in them is very painful to them. It is a terrible torment, next to which the worse sufferings of our life on this earth are nothing. Beneath the action of the divine fire that eliminates the crust, the souls do not acquire a splendor superior to that which they already possess on entering purgatory, but their splendor is veiled by the crust. Then my guardian angel said to me:

The souls in purgatory are fixed in their degree of holiness and of perfection which will be theirs for eternity in heaven, and which is, in some way, the

---

[26] The sufferings of purgatory are voluntary, for the soul looks upon them as a means of glorifying God, paying its debt to divine justice, and attaining the beatific vision, the desire for which consumes it. The soul knows that the pain that it is suffering is purifying and that it will have an end. It is in peace, abandoned into the hands of God (see St. Thomas Aquinas, *Summa Theologica*, Supplement, q. 70, ter., a. 4).

degree of their level of glory in heaven: there is in
them no moral stain, no impurity; they are con-
firmed in grace and impeccable.[27]

Afterward I had another vision: I saw the souls in purgatory immersed in a fire, in a vivid light, and in a fiery
wave that was bursting over them. The angel explained
to me:

The souls are submerged in the flames of love.
They are united in this fire in the divine charity
that attracts them, inflames them, and illuminates
them: Purgatory is the kingdom of divine charity.
By this immersion in divine love, the souls are
surrendered to charity, which they exercise with
perfection both toward God and among them-
selves, and also toward you on earth. In the light of
divine love, they know each other, and they know
themselves to be united and drawn to God. And
in this light, God communicates himself to them,
increasing their happiness and attracting them
toward the Beatific Vision. This fire of love, this
light of divine charity, is truly sanctifying because
it opens the souls little by little to the fulfillment of
God's desire for them.

---

[27] Let us recall briefly the teaching of the Church on this point: The souls
in purgatory are sure of their salvation. Their heaven is assured, but in
the other life they now cannot merit (a very certain truth recalled by Pope
Leo X, in answer to Luther). In purgatory, souls act freely and are not
in a state of numbness (Declaration of the Holy Office against Rosmini,
December 14, 1887, D.T.C., art. Purgatorio, col. 1298), nor do they have
any feelings of anxiety or horror (Leo X against Luther).

I contemplated these blessed souls who are suffering for love, who are all-saturated with God and all-faithful. I saw them, not in a hierarchy, but in an order and an incomparable unity; there were among them neither superiors nor inferiors because all of them submit with great joy and a living sorrow to the love of God and his pure will. My angel then told me:

> *The souls in purgatory are at the same time in fire and light—burned by the fire of love, they give themselves to love, and they live this gift of love in a great mutual charity. They pray because prayer is the perfect expression of love. They pray for each other, they pray for you, and they pray for their benefactors. Their prayer is focused on the sole glorification of God and his love, not on their own needs. They do not pray to be liberated from purgatory, but rather that God be glorified by their liberation. They do not pray for the conversion of sinners on earth nor for the sanctification of souls, but that God be glorified in these conversions and sanctifications. One must never lose sight of the fact that the souls in purgatory do not have any self-interest or any interest in created things. Their gaze is united and purified in God, and in him and for him they permit themselves at times to contemplate the rest . . .*

The angel stated this teaching more precisely, explaining the marvels of divine love:

> *Charity is no more than the exercise on the part of man of the love of God that is poured out on him,*

*which is surrendered to him, which illuminates
him. You are often not sure of this great reality:
but the souls in purgatory, who have great knowledge, know this very well; they love you perfectly,
and they truly love each other because they only
love God. They love you in God and for God. This
is true love: simple, disinterested, pure, and true.
In finding themselves in this perfect perception of
love, they are grateful to those who pray for them
and those who bring consolation to them. Don't
ever forget that love for one's neighbor comes from
love of God. But often men invent expressions of
love; they disfigure the gift of God, appropriating
it for themselves. But only God is the source of all
love, because he is love.*

Love is a gift of God, a divine deposit in us. The love
of God is the first thing; it is given to us as a token that we
have to bear fruit and constantly return to the One who
has granted it to us first. My angel then told me:

*The souls in purgatory find themselves in the light of
divine love. They have great knowledge, more rapid
and more complete than all you can have on earth.
They know in an immediate way, as spirits do—by
intuition and immediate communication—certain
realities and mysteries. They know the mystery of
death because they have experienced it; they know
the mystery of eternity and the immortality of the
soul, which they are experiencing right now. Beyond
the knowledge of faith, they know the existence of
God, the Virgin Mary, the saints, and the angels.*

They receive great intellectual lights—they know themselves in the light of divine love, and they recognize themselves as humble sinners, objects of the justice and mercy of God.

They know the love of God perfectly, and they recognize their lack of this love, their state, and their expiation. All of their knowledge leads them to surrender themselves more fully to this love that acts in them—to accept it with great patience, to give thanks by prayer, and to favor its extension by all means.

Everything seemed to me so clear, so transparent. How many vain, superfluous questions vanished then! God is so simple, so uncomplicated! My holy angel spoke again.

The souls in purgatory are in a state of need and receptivity: They are equally dedicated to the love of God. This double state, as paradoxical as it appears, is the consequence of the fire of love of purgatory, a fire that attracts them in their pain and in their happiness. Their pain calls out for relief, their happiness for a giving of self. Yes, the souls in purgatory are very much in need; they are very receptive to your prayers, which relieve them a great deal, and they are dedicated to their own prayer, which pays homage and praise to the glory of God.

The souls in purgatory are doubly submitted to love since they are submissive to the exercise in themselves of the mercy and the justice of God. Justice is exercised in them in this exigency of expiation of the debt of their sin. As far as mercy is concerned, this is exercised also under this demand because love imposes on these souls a limited and finite expiation for sin (which is an infinite offense).

In purgatory you will always see both the light of mercy and the fire of justice. Purgatory is a reality that is at the same time both terrible and consoling. One must not separate these two characteristics when one speaks of purgatory. . . .

Do you understand how much you have to pray for the holy souls in purgatory? This is very much forgotten today; there are few people who think of this; there are very few priests who pray and offer Masses for these holy souls. Therefore you must write to awaken this concern for the souls in purgatory, and you must remind your brothers that the communion of saints is a reality with its demands of charity.[28] Then, my child, pray and ask others to pray for the holy souls in purgatory.

After this, the angel disappeared from my view, leaving me in an act of thanksgiving and with an extraordinary joy.

---

[28] See CCC, 1032: "From the beginning the Church has honored the memory of the dead and offered prayers in suffrage for them, above all the Eucharistic sacrifice, so that, thus purified, they may attain the beatific vision of God. The Church also commends almsgiving, indulgences, and works of penance undertaken on behalf of the dead:

"Let us help and commemorate them. If Job's sons were purified by their father's sacrifice, why would we doubt that our offerings for the dead bring them some consolation? Let us not hesitate then, to help those who have died and to offer our prayers for them" (St. John Chrysostom, *Hom in 1 Cor.* 41, 5: PG 61, 361; see Job 1:5).

THE EXERCISE OF FAITH IN PURGATORY

Morning prayer. My soul was happy in the immensity of divine love, an ocean of indescribable softness in which I lost myself totally. In this sea of fire, of love, of light, my soul was possessed by God, drawn by him, and rested in him with an ineffable joy. I was not thinking or reflecting; I handed myself over and let myself be possessed, and he filled me with his love. At the same time I suffered a piercing pain, as though my soul had been cut in two. I was wounded and frustrated, feeling confusedly the limitations of this weakness and my incapacity to fully possess this love although I touched it in some way. After this, I saw myself in God. My soul was submerged in the fire of Jesus' heart. I contemplated how his infinite love flowed over the whole Church. A double current of water and of blood bathed, vivified, and inflamed ceaselessly the Church militant and the souls in purgatory. It seemed to me that heaven was also the Most Sacred Heart of Jesus. Jesus asked me to offer such graces—at the same time, soft, ardent, and painful—for the holy souls in purgatory, uniting myself to them. I protested, saying, "Why, Lord? Blessed are these souls in purgatory for whom you ask me to offer this love. They suffer a great deal, but at least they possess you, and that cannot be snatched away anymore."

Then our Lord asked me if I preferred to know the pains, the sufferings, and the joys of purgatory or snatches of passing ecstasies. I did not know how to answer him. He told me that for three days my soul would be submerged in the state of purgatory. That realization was an

unprecedented torture. I enjoyed God in a kind of perception, an intellectual possession that was incomplete and
heartbreaking. I seemed to possess him as though through
a mysterious veil—a gift of love that made me tremble.
For a day, my soul was in a state of burning pain; I found
myself in front of a curtain of light, behind which was the
object of my love, desiring to give himself and extending his arms to me, without my having any possibility of
reaching him. During this whole day my soul was favored
with various visits from the Immaculate Virgin, my guardian angel, my friends in heaven—my holy patrons and
protectors—and my deceased relatives who were now in
paradise. They came to me through this veil of light; they
visited me and spoke to me of the divine love with great
ardor and joy. My soul was tortured by desire for this love,
and I had an overwhelming desire to see this veil of light
finally torn apart to reveal love in its fullness so I could
attain it and enjoy him.

During every moment of that day, I thought I would
die as a result of this burning desire. My soul felt like it
was being torn apart and left in pieces. It seemed to me
that in this state, the veil of faith was torn and my soul
gained access to many hidden realities. But I did not see
God—I only perceived his mysterious presence as beyond
a veil. At the end of the day, my guardian angel came to me
and said:

> *Look my child! The Most High has permitted you
> to know this mystery and experience in your soul
> the condition of the blessed souls in purgatory. He
> also wants to teach you and arouse your unfailing*

prayer for the holy souls in purgatory. In purgatory, faith subsists in part since it has not yet been replaced by the beatific vision.

You have seen clearly that the souls in purgatory do not see God; they perceive him only in his mysterious presence. At the moment of death, the veil of faith is not completely torn except for those souls introduced instantly into the glory of the vision of the face of God.

For those who have to go to purgatory, faith still subsists partially.[29] *But these holy souls in purgatory have an experiential knowledge of many supernatural realities that remain as mysteries of faith for us here on earth.*

They experience their own immortality; they are in eternity. . . . They enjoy the effects of the communion of saints; they see the Virgin Mary and the angels and saints; they know that heaven and hell exist.

---

[29] In purgatory the soul is in a state of completion insofar as it is not able to merit or increase its charity. But it is also "underway," *in statu viae, aliquo modo* (*Summa Theologica* Supplement, q. 70 ter., a. 6 ad 5). It does not yet possess the eternal beatitude to which God destines it. It does not see God face-to-face, but it comes closer and closer to God. It has a clear vision of certain realities that are hidden from us here on earth behind the veil of faith. Not having the vision of God, there is in these souls a sufficient obscurity to give room for faith. The formal object of that faith is the "first truth, insofar as it escapes our vision" (*Summa Theologica*, IIa IIae q. 4, a. 1). Under this aspect, the soul in purgatory still possesses faith. It adheres to the first truth without seeing it, but it believes in it. The way of faith in purgatory differs from the way of faith on earth; it is, in fact, a faith without merit. The soul in purgatory adheres to the divine truth under the power of an immutable will because such a soul is no longer subject to free will.

But they do not see God, whom they do not yet possess; on this point, faith is still exercised by the souls in purgatory.

Yet their intellect no longer has any doubt; their will is fixed in the divine will, and they have no doubts. These holy souls are submerged in a contemplative prayer, in a humble and reverential fear of God, whom they know is present but whom they do not see. And it is this painful hope of seeing God, to possess him fully at last, that inflames their desire and causes their suffering.

After having asked me to pray even more for these holy souls in purgatory and to offer for that intention this grace of three days that had been conceded to me by God, the angel disappeared from my view.

THE EXERCISE OF HOPE IN PURGATORY

After my morning prayer, my soul was submerged again in this state of purgatory. It seemed to me that the inferior part of my soul was almost dead: I say almost, since I continued to be occupied more or less with my usual activities. I had the impression of seeing my soul cut in two, torn apart. God allowed himself to be perceived through the veil of light I mentioned yesterday, but without my possessing or reaching him. He enflamed my soul with the most burning desires, to the point that, at midday, I had to lie down because my body could no longer resist these outbursts of love. My soul savored the firstfruits of this future union with God; it was a gentleness so exquisite and so painful that I was felt faint. My soul, as if thrown into a bonfire, remained in peace, although I suffered continuously.

During that day, I was subject to an unheard of dryness and bitterness, and I was incapable of any other activity except a great sorrow for all my faults. I experienced a kind of interior confession during which all my sins were revealed to me, one after another, by the hundreds and thousands. During this day I relived my entire life down to the smallest details, with the smallest faults, the grave faults, the doubts, the complacencies, and the negligences. Seeing each fault was like my soul being whipped, and I cried interiorly: "Oh, my God! How little have I cared for your glory, and how I have wasted your graces!"

My soul remained, however, in a great yet painful peace. I did not fear being the object of God's reprobation, since it seemed to me then that the most important thing was his glory. I had a devouring thirst for this glory and wanted to remain in this state of torture for as long as necessary for God to be glorified. This profound grace of interior confession has been an enormous, unprecedented blessing for my soul. This was added to all that had been granted to me on the previous day. I believe that God held back and made those states known to me partially in a successive way, since human nature here below could not have withstood this any other way.

Throughout the day, the bodily suffering continued, but my soul was immersed in a vivid peace; it was inflamed with desire, peaceful and yet dying. Each visit of the Blessed Virgin and the angels and the saints overwhelmed me, because it inflamed my desire and caused me to contemplate all that was promised to me, for which I yearned with all the strength of my soul linked to the pure will of God. I remained here, in calm abandonment to the will of God, with neither hurry nor impatience, desiring only the glory of God. The only words I could utter, which all the celestial visitors repeated, were:

Glory, glory, glory,
God is the Holy of Holies,
Glory, glory, glory!

This increased my pain, increased my desire for God, intensified an extraordinary serenity, and literally saturated my soul. In the paradox of this thirst for the glory of God, I saw my holy guardian angel, stern and resplendent. He said to me in a grave tone:

You are experiencing now the great mystery of
purgatory, that which in some way is the mystery
of hope.[30]
This serene hope that you feel is the same as the
souls feel toward the Most High: a purifying and
painful hope for the soul desiring the full revelation
of God face-to-face.
In purgatory hope is totally simplified until it
disappears in a radical hope of God, a pure and

---

[30] Hope, as St. Thomas Aquinas says, makes us tend to God, as to a good to be obtained finally, and as to a helper strong to assist us (*Summa Theologica* IIa IIae, q. 17, a. 6 ad 3). In purgatory the soul still does not enjoy eternal happiness, toward which it tends ardently as toward a future and possible good. The soul in purgatory hopes for the infinite good from God, which consists in the eternal enjoyment of God. It bases its hope on the divine mercy that makes this good possible. It waits for *nothing less than God through God*, thus exercising the virtue of hope in a perfect way.

disinterested hope in which there is no precipita-
tion, nor impatience, nor calculation—it is a pure
waiting for the hour of God, a very painful hope!

In this perfect hope, the soul remains invariably
serene; it is submerged in a painful quietude. The
certainty of its salvation provokes in it an ardent
desire and a burning hope that consumes it. This
hope is the very state of purgatory, which has no
other objective than God and no other desire than
his glory. In purgatory the souls know that the
moment of their liberation is fixed by divine mercy
itself, which God's justice has established for the
greater glory of the Most High. Therefore they are
in peace, the very peace of God.

I then found myself in purgatory, in the fire itself, in
accord with the promises of the Lord to my soul. I know
that I have experienced all this as an effect of his infinite
love; I experienced it in my soul removed from my body,
which was bent under the force of grace and could not
resist. After this moment, I did not recover consciousness,
but my soul, as though suddenly freed from its attachment
to the body, was launched into the ocean of divine love.

THE EXERCISE OF CHARITY IN PURGATORY

Fire and ardent prayer, ablaze! Until now I had known a
great light and an ineffable peace, but now my soul was
submerged by the grace of God in a fire of devouring love.
My holy angel was with me, and I said to him: "At last it
has been accomplished. When will I enter into heaven?"

He did not answer me, and I sighed. Around me were thousands of souls burning with love. A gentle light surrounded us like a vehement fire. I was in total joy, and my happiness increased even more when the angel said to me:

> *This is the antechamber of heaven; it is the fulfillment of purgatory. And here is where souls are submerged in the pure attraction of divine Love.*
>
> *Here also is where the sufferings are most vivid and most intense.*

What happiness! Here souls are suffering for love; they suffer *from* love, for here is the promise of love. There is a great cloud shining above these souls to which they are at times elevated, and there are explosions of happiness and jubilation in purgatory. These souls are ascending to the beatific vision; they are entering heaven! They suffer from love, and they ardently love this suffering. The soul completely transported by love is subjected to a loving impatience to see God and possess him. It sighs, languishing with love. It cannot express this love more than as a burning prayer of thanksgiving, jubilation, praise to the holiness of God, to his mercy which has saved it, and to his justice which has purified it. My soul could not experience this mystery of charity in purgatory more than in a global, general way. The angel explained this great charity in purgatory:

> *In purgatory, the holy souls are inundated by the love of God, and they enjoy this infinite love. They are turned toward God, they love him perfectly, and they show this in their gratitude:*

They give thanks for having been saved, having been confirmed in grace, and being from now on impeccable, capable of giving glory to God in spirit and in truth.

This causes them a marvelous jubilation; they are snatched up by love. Only in heaven will they enjoy this love in its radiant fullness, in an intimate union with God who is love. But there still exists this desire in purgatory that impedes the plenitude of love; in heaven there is no longer any more desire—it is the possession of love.

I saw this love scorching the holy souls; this very fire of purgatory is the divine love that invades everything. In purgatory the souls are all dedicated to divine love; they are, so to speak, like embers scorched by the love of God, but they are not consumed by this love. Purgatory is, in a certain way, the love of God that does not consume, that finishes its work in the souls surrendered to him.

I also saw that the souls in purgatory love God and their neighbor much more perfectly than we do here on earth. They love God above all else—God in himself, for himself—and they love us in him, because they see us as objects of his infinite love. They love us in a living light of truth and purity. Here below, as a general rule we love more easily our brethren first, and afterward God in them, because we are very limited by our weaknesses, our sensitivities, and our lack of faith. The love we give to our neighbor should be a manifestation of the love we have for God, and we cannot measure our love other than with the manifestation of our love for our neighbor.

In purgatory, "You shall love the Lord your God . . ." is the first commandment. "You shall love your neighbor as yourself" is the second commandment.[31] The holy souls in purgatory love one another in God, and they love us in God; they are closely united to us by this love. To manifest their love toward God and toward the other souls in purgatory and toward the Church militant, they pray. They pray for each other, rejoicing in seeing that this or that soul has ended its punishment and entered heaven. They pray for the dead who arrive in purgatory and for us here below. They intercede for us as much as God permits; they assist and help us. The prayer of the souls in purgatory is intense, continuous, and gratuitous: they can no longer merit for themselves or for others.[32]

Purgatory is a world of prayer, and prayer is a language of love; therefore, purgatory is a world of love. It is established in peace, harmony, and order, which are fruits of God's love. The souls there are all surrendered to the pure will of God, which is love. And because love reigns in purgatory, I could say that there is no greater joy—except that of heaven—than finding oneself in purgatory. I contemplated this world of love and of prayer where all the holy souls, before all else, pray to God to glorify him, giving testimony with gratitude and praying for us. Such are the great truths that were revealed to me this day. I

---

[31] Matthew 22:37–39.

[32] "The souls in purgatory are not . . . isolated, not only because they have a relationship with the faithful on earth and with the elect in heaven, but also because they live in society, they know each other, they love each other and help one another as brothers and sisters" (P. Martin Jugie in J. Joubert and L. Cristiani, *Les plus beaux textes*, 223).

returned to myself, my body broken and exhausted, but my soul still invaded by love.

THE PRAYER OF THE SOULS IN PURGATORY

My guardian angel approached me and said with great gravity:

> *Pray often for the souls in purgatory, who are praying so much for you.*[33]

---

[33] Do the souls in purgatory pray for us? To this question, St. Thomas Aquinas and St. Robert Bellarmine, both doctors of the Church, answered differently. St. Thomas distinguished three states the souls of the just might be in after death:

- the saints, who are "in their homeland," know in the Word everything that concerns them and all the prayers of men who have recourse to them (*Summa Theologica* III. q. 10, a. 2); it is proper to them, says Cajetan, to see the prayers that we send to them (ibid., IIa IIae q. 83, a. 11, no. 1).

- The saints who are in the old limbo can also pray for the living, because they are not in a penal state similar to that of the souls in purgatory, who, by their fault, are dependent on the prayers of the Church militant. They are in a state superior to ours, not only by reason of their impeccability (like the souls in purgatory), but also due to the aspect of independence. Thus they can ask the saints who are in the homeland to pray for the living. This is why it says in Scripture that the saints pray for us. St. Thomas cites (ibid., IIa IIae, q. 83, a. 11 *sed Contra*) the apparition of Jeremiah to Judas Maccabeus: "This is the friend of your brethren who prays much for the people and for the holy city, Jeremiah, the prophet of God" (2 Maccabees 15:14). The saints of the old limbo, who still did not have the vision of God, prayed for the living without being able to know, as opposed to the saints in Heaven, of the prayers of the living. Scripture, observes Cajetan, affirms that Jeremiah prayed, but it does not say that he heard the prayers of the living. If one admits that he knew of the trials and prayers of Judas Maccabeus, one has to say, with John of St. Thomas, that it was in virtue of an exceptional divine revelation (see *De Oratione*, disp. 14, no. 441).

They are very much forgotten; too many people forget their duty to pray for them; too many people show themselves ungrateful.

With a gesture of his hand, he made me see very clearly the holy souls in purgatory submerged in the constant fire of infinite love, and I contemplated their prayer. For many years, I did not know that the souls in purgatory were praying for us; this idea had never occurred to me. I believed that they were just suffering their punishment, and nothing more. Nevertheless, their very intense prayer

---

- The souls in purgatory are superior to us, says St. Thomas Aquinas, in the sense that they are confirmed in grace and are impeccable. But they are inferior because of the personal punishment that they have to suffer at the tribunal of divine justice, which places them in dependence on our prayers. Before the souls in purgatory pray for us, we have to pray for them (see *Summa Theologica*, IIa IIae q. 83, a. 2, ad 3).

St. Robert Bellarmine, who emphasizes less the penal character of purgatory, does not distinguish more than two states of the just souls after death (see *De Ecclesia quae est in Purgatorio* lib. II, ch. 15):

- The saints in their homeland who pray for us and know of our prayers.
- The saints in the ancient limbo and the souls in purgatory, who according to St. Robert Bellarmine, belong to a single state, pray for us, but without knowing of our prayers. He did not establish a distinction, with respect to the possibility of praying, between the saints in limbo and the souls in purgatory. He cited the text of 2 Maccabees 15:14 to establish that the souls in purgatory pray for us. And this opinion of St. Robert Bellarmine is shared by Suarez, who without considering it certain, considered it pious and probable.

In the opinion of Dante, in Canto XI of *Purgatorio*, where the poet presents us to the souls capable of praying expressly for the living, he says they no longer pray for their fellows who are confirmed in grace and now don't need it, but for those who are still on earth, and he does this paraphrasing the last petition of the Our Father: "Don't let them enter into temptation" (see Cardinal Journet, "*Le Purgatoire*" in Études Religieuses, 301–302 [*La Pensée Catholique*, 1932]).

is very different from ours. It is incomparably more beautiful and richer in harmony and unity, for it is not mixed as
ours is with any kind of feelings or sensibility.

This prayer of the souls in purgatory is like a surging
of divine charity that completely clothes them, consuming
them with love. They pray at the same time with great joy
and great pain. I believe that no one can truly have an idea
of their state, other than St. Paul who said that he exulted
with joy in his tribulations and trials.

The holy souls in purgatory pray constantly, in a serene
and disinterested supplication: what they receive of the
divine love that fills them, they want to give to others.
They never want to keep anything for themselves because
they are only interested in giving glory to God. And the
glory of God is the expansion of infinite love in all souls;
it is the expansion of the kingdom of God. They have an
extreme compassion for their fellow men who are with
them, as well as for all the persons whom they knew here
below and all members of the Church militant whose eternal salvation they desire with ardor and love so that God
be glorified. They pray for all of this. Afterward the angel
spoke to me of what he called "the liturgy of purgatory."

*The blessed souls of purgatory are in constant
prayer; everything in them is prayer, because they
are completely surrendered to the pure will of God.
        They unite in a special way to all of the litur-
gical celebrations on earth, and these feasts of the
Church mark a certain rhythm, although they no
longer know the measure of time. The liturgy of the
souls in purgatory is based on the adoration of the*

*justice and the sanctity of God and is closely mod-
eled on the liturgical manifestations of the Church
militant.*

*Their prayer is a very pure adoration, united to
the praise of thanksgiving that they raise constantly
to the Most High for their salvation. They celebrate
the mercies of the Lord.*

*They pray for each other, but not for themselves,
since they are all snatched up into the pure will of
God and they are totally forgetful of themselves.*

*But they implore without ceasing the liberation
of the others because they burn with charity for
one another and of zeal for the glory of God. They
know that every soul's liberation from purgatory
contributes to the glory of God, and this glorification of God is their only preoccupation.*

*Freed from all obstacles of sensibility and of
concupiscence, these holy souls can pray for one
another in the light of a perfect love.*

*On some feasts, especially those of the Most
Blessed Virgin, many souls are liberated: this is an
occasion of great joy for all of purgatory. Every
Mass also brings to these souls many consolations,
especially those celebrated for their intention and
particularly those on November 2. The souls do
not cease to give thanks to God and to pray for the
intentions of those who pray for them: they are
assiduous in praying to God for the conversion and
the sanctification of all mankind, and they also*

*direct themselves to the Blessed Mother of God and
to the saints to ask their intercession for all of you
who are still on earth.*

*This is the great prayer of the souls in purgatory, who
are nourished at the fire of divine charity and who
exercise themselves for the glory of God, the extension of his kingdom, and the salvation of all souls.*

When the angel had explained these things to me,
everything disappeared from my interior sight and I
remained in prayer.

A WORLD OF PRAYER

Morning prayer. In a vivid interior light, my soul was invited
to contemplate the prayer of the holy souls in purgatory.
I saw them engulfed in a humble availability to the pure
divine will. Their prayer rose in spirals toward the throne
of God like the smoke of incense with three reflections, or
colors. My guardian angel, who was close to me, told me:

*Look, my child, and understand well. This image
shows you the prayer of the holy souls, and
explains to you its three characteristics; for that
reason you see the smoke of incense that rises in
spirals of three different colors.*

There were, in effect, very light white spirals, heavier spirals of a vivid red, and very heavy spirals of a golden color,
but it was one and the same smoke. The angel continued:

*The prayer of the holy souls in purgatory is per-
fectly humble, perfectly trusting, and perfectly*

grateful. It is above all a prayer of thanksgiving,
incessantly glorifying the holiness of God. The
souls are ecstatic in this contemplation by absolute
choice: they know that they will see God face-to-
face, and they remain prostrate before his holiness
in an attitude of profound humility. They know
they are unworthy of his mercy, and they know
that this painful purification will finally make
them capable of possessing God.

I contemplated these souls, who seemed to me to be
overwhelmed in their misery, confounded by finding
themselves so unworthy before the divine sanctity and by
being the objects of the burning love of God. They are in
a very painful fire that captivates and surrounds them. In
some way, it is as if this fire limits and opposes their normal spiritual activity. Thus, they surrender themselves very
docilely to the pure divine will, submitting to it in an attitude of profound humility that prevents them from having the least interest in themselves. They do not pray for
themselves—they expiate, they pray for others, and above
all, they pray to glorify God.

They are very stable, serene, and trusting because they
have been despoiled of every kind of false limitation and
the shackles of a sensible, affective, psychological order.
There is neither fear nor doubt nor uncertainty in them,
but instead a soft, gentle peace and certainty, and this saturates their prayer with a great confidence and power. My
holy angel said to me:

The holy souls in purgatory are strong because they
are in peace. Their union with the divine will is

*already so total and perfect that they obtain from it
a great patience and a radical confidence.*

*Also their prayer is trusting; they express the
hope of fully enjoying their salvation in the eternal
possession of God, whom they love. These souls
still lack knowledge, but they know that they are,
from now on, saved from any fault or error. And
thus they have perfect confidence.*

I saw them, above all, in an incessant happiness and an
unspeakable joy that literally elevates them toward God,
and their strong yearnings of love turns them toward all
the members of the holy Church. The angel told me:

*Their yearnings are the yearnings of thanksgiving,
since the blessed souls have intense joy in the midst
of the most vivid sufferings. They feel the joy and
the happiness of being saved forever, and they are
continuously thankful for this gift of salvation.*

*They give thanks without ceasing to God for
all the graces that he has given them in this state
of purgatory: their knowledge is greater and more
complete than yours is on earth, and they savor
certain mysteries that for you are still a matter
of faith because they experience and know them
firsthand. They receive innumerable aid from all
the Church in heaven and on earth. These are the
effects of the unbreakable communion of the saints,
and they give thanks to the Most High in perpetual
outbursts of gratitude.*

*Observe how the prayer of the souls in purgatory
is beautiful, pure, serene, and so perfect! These are*

*the joys of purgatory. This does not exclude in any
way their pain and suffering, but they are like lights
in the night, testimonies of the infinite love of God.*

I contemplated these perfumed spirals of smoke rising
toward the throne of God that transmit the overwhelming intensity of prayer in purgatory. Purgatory is a world
of prayer—for the souls there, prayer is the language of
charity, and they are immersed in the burning love of God.
Then everything vanished from my interior gaze. O my
God, if we could only pray like that, with as much fervor
and love as the holy souls of purgatory!

A SEVENFOLD SOURCE OF HAPPINESS AND JOY

Evening prayer. I saw purgatory as a globe of fire in which
there was a perpetual and intense movement. This was a
precise and clear intellectual vision. I contemplated this
burning globe that moved without ceasing, where the souls
seemed to be immersed and enclosed. There were, from
time to time, some who arose like blazing stars to ascend
to heaven in a great light; others, on the contrary, like dark
comets descended from earth to incorporate themselves in
this globe, from which they arose later, radiant, to ascend
to heaven . . .

I saw this globe bathed in a torrent of very soft light,
which poured forth in great waves from the Eucharistic
Heart of Jesus. This was like an infinite river of divine
charity. It surrounded and penetrated the globe, and therefore purgatory, and saturated it, extending outward in
seven rivers of love that are the fruitful plenitude of divine
charity in purgatory.

In purgatory itself, where the souls find themselves maintained in the bosom of divine charity that purifies them, I saw the seven rivers as a sevenfold source of happiness and joy endlessly unfolding. It was very beautiful and consoling. I understood how the souls in purgatory find themselves totally immersed in divine charity, and how they exercise the joy of divine love there. This profound happiness of the holy souls in purgatory is a burning flame that burns and illuminates them in order to purify them and fully unite them to God.

First I saw how these blessed souls are united in God's love by a tender charity and a very delicate compassion that incites them constantly to pray for each other in a completely disinterested way. They rejoice in the departure of one or another to heaven, and they maintain an ardent compassion for those who arrive from earthly life, dividing up the suffrages that await them. It is very touching! This gives an example of what our fraternal charity should be here below.[34]

---

[34] Their reverence toward divine holiness is without measure, and it is what one can conceive as most fundamental in their state. They are united and unite themselves incessantly among themselves with links of love and fire, on the altar of sanctity immolating themselves in his honor. Their state, their life, their whole being is a gentle, full, and perpetual echo of the song that is never interrupted in heaven: "Holy, holy, holy is the Lord God of hosts," which is the basis for a symphony. This melody, so grave and constant in its living hymn, is so in the universal concert that sanctified creation dedicates to God. They have an ineffable joy, seeing that God is such a holy light, that the very shadow of a shadow impedes union with him. This evidence makes them rejoice much more than their sufferings afflict them. And they don't in any way want this suffering to be less intense or less lasting than it should be. If they ask to be liberated, at times insistently, it is much more out of love for God than to be freed from their punishment (Msgr. Gay, in J. Joubert and L. Cristiani, *Les plus beaux textes*, 219).

Afterward, I was able to contemplate the extreme happiness of the souls in purgatory in the midst of the light of divine love. They no longer have any doubt nor fear; they do not know anxiety or temptation. They are definitely freed, not only from sin, but also from all temptation. They are thus assured of no longer offending God. They are able to glorify him and enjoy the experience they have of his holiness, although it comes through the burning rigors of their state. All of this is for them a cause of great joy.

I also saw that the holy souls have the happiness, the gentle ineffable joy, of possessing God as through a veil and experiencing a great number of consoling mysteries, such as that of immortality, eternal life, and the communion of saints. These mysteries are revealed to them in multiple forms, and they can apprehend them interiorly, which is a source of great joy for them.[35]

---

[35] Richard of St. Victor (+1173) spoke of the "joys of purgatory." He wrote in *Grades of Charity:* "The soul in purgatory has reached the perfection of charity. God lets his presence be felt in such a form, but he does not show anything of his face. He interiorly pours out his sweetness, but does not show his beauty. He pours out gentleness, but does not show his light. They feel then his sweetness, but they do not see his charms. He is surrounded by clouds and obscurity. His throne is still upon a clouded column. The truth is that what they see is extremely sweet and caressing; but all is in darkness, because our Lord has not yet appeared in light. The fire warms more than it illuminates. It inflames the will well, but it does not illuminate the understanding; the soul in this state can sense its Beloved well, but is not allowed to perceive him. If he sees him, it is as though in the night; as behind a cloud. Finally the soul sees well, as in a mirror, in an enigma, but not face to face; hence there comes his cry:

"Let the light of your countenance shine upon your servant!" (J. Joubert and L. Cristiani, *Les plus beaux textes*, 201).

Another cause of happiness for these holy souls is receiving the suffrages of the Church militant in the liturgy—which they are united to in a way that is appropriate for them—participating and obtaining great consolations that are constantly renewed. They pray with perfect purity of intention for the conversion and sanctification of all men and women and for the extension of the kingdom of God, whose glory is their only aspiration. And since these blessed souls have no other desire than the glory of God, this prayer is as pure and perfect as it is fruitful and efficacious.

The joy of hope is ineffable: the certainty of being saved and from then on contributing to the glory of God. The souls in purgatory experience a radiant hope that we are incapable of conceiving; it is so calm, powerful, disinterested, and pure. It is a source of new joys and a river of acts of thanksgiving that they continue without ceasing. These blessed souls are submerged in hope, which is their permanent state. It is an intense joy for them; they perceive what they are going to possess, as an effect of the mercy of God in them, and they have no fear of losing it, nor any impetuous impatience to attain it. In a gentle happiness in the midst of their sufferings, they hope in God.[36]

---

[36] While they are subject to suffering that human words cannot describe, the Church in purgatory has its heart elevated by an inexhaustible joy, because it knows with supernatural certainty that it is saved forever, and that each moment of remaining in its state brings it closer to that ineffable instant when the glory of God will appear and all its desires will be satisfied. This is the common teaching of theologians, and St. Robert Bellarmine notes that the sureness the Church suffering enjoys, without excluding hope, excludes every shadow of fear of sin and of eternal condemnation. They still lack the certainty that the Church glorious gives, where the elect have no fear, nor even hope, because they already have the possession. But

I also saw a more delicate, exquisite joy: that of the numerous visits made by the Most Blessed Virgin, the angels, and all the saints to the souls in purgatory to alleviate their pain, encourage them, strengthen them, and finally free them when God permits—or more exactly, escort them and accompany them when the hour of their liberation arrives. These holy souls savor the joy of being loved personally and the power of being grateful for the infinite goodness of God and all the inhabitants of the celestial Jerusalem, beginning with the Virgin Mary, Queen of heaven and earth. I have seen how a single visit of the Immaculate Virgin Mary lights up all of purgatory. All the souls, including the most abandoned, benefit and receive consolation, whether it is from seeing some of them consoled, or whether it is the simple intervention of the Blessed Virgin who announces their future liberation to them.

In the midst of all these joys, a more specific and more general happiness arises, surrounding in some manner all of the others. It is the primary joy of purgatory—that of being abandoned to the pure will of God, not wanting anything other than what he wants and therefore obedient to the realization of his pure divine will. This is wonderful! I have been shown that all the souls in purgatory savor more or less this sevenfold joy, and that the minimal participation of the soul in one or another is incomparably more sweet and attractive than all that we know as most

---

it is a security much higher than that of the Church militant, where the just have no more than the certainty of hope respecting their eternal salvation, which cannot exclude all reason for fear" (Cardinal Journet, *Le Purgatoire*, 301–302).

exquisite here below. The most lasting and even the most intense moments of joy here on earth are nothing in comparison with the smallest joy in purgatory.[37]

This interior vision has been an inestimable grace and indescribable consolation for my soul. It is good that we know how much the holy souls in purgatory suffer, and this should incite us above all to pray for them and not forget them, but it is also advisable for us to know their joys, to give thanks to God, and to contribute with our prayers and our suffrages. The vision of their happiness, which is so pure and supernatural, should inflame our hearts with love and gratitude toward God and confirm us in an unbreakable hope. Can I ever thank our Lord for all this magnanimity of his infinite love that

---

[37] A gentle security, unknown on earth, fills the Church of purgatory with a happiness that surpasses all understanding: "I do not believe," says St. Catherine of Genoa, "that one could find a happiness on earth comparable to what a soul in purgatory enjoys, aside from that which the saints feel in paradise. And each day that happiness increases, by the influence that God exercises on that soul. This joy grows to the extent that the dominant impediment is consumed: the impediment is nothing other than the crust of sin. The fire consumes it and at the same time the soul discovers, more and more, the divine influence. It's like something covered that could never respond to the reverberation of the sun; not because of any defect in the sun, which shines without ceasing, but because of the obstacle that is formed by the cover that is on top of the thing. If the cover disappears, the sun is presented, and the more it disappears, the more the object will respond to the rays of the sun. Thus the rust, that is to say the punishment of sin, is the cover over the soul; it is consumed in purgatory as a result of the fire, and the more it is consumed, the more the soul corresponds to God, who is the true sun. In the measure that the rust diminishes, the soul is exposed to the divine rays and its happiness increases. In this way, happiness grows and the punishment of sin is erased, until the time when it is completed" (see Cardinal Journet, *Le Purgatoire*, 301–302).

he dispenses freely to my misery? He has allowed me to glimpse the reflection of his love, his infinite goodness, in the mystery of purgatory. He is always watching over us, like a loving Father. And these supernatural realities, with which he has nourished our souls, will be for us the object of a faithful and loving contemplation, a spiritual enrichment, and an occasion to pray and give thanks. For this reason he wants these things to be written and known. He has put in my path a holy priest, a very good father and a man of prayer. By this spiritual paternity, by this firm and good direction, God has guided me. He has also allowed these great realities of purgatory to be received in prayer and written down in spite of my initial repugnance in doing this. Now I do it with pleasure, since I know that it is for God's glory and for the good of souls—above all for those souls in purgatory. Would that these writings contribute to making these souls more loved and prayed for! Then the will of God would be fulfilled. That is what my guardian angel said to me one day in regard to a severe and overwhelming vision of purgatory.

Child, abide in God's peace. You must write all that will be shown to you. It is for the glory of the Most High. Obedience demands it, so do it. The glory of God demands it, even though you do not understand it. These writings can do much good for souls; they can incite them to pray more for the souls in purgatory.

If you knew that just one soul in purgatory could be freed thanks to these writings, you would

*not hesitate. . . . Then write out of love and obe-
dience. All this is given to you for the Holy Church:
Do not guard it avariciously; do not lock up in
your hands this gift of God! Be a small instrument,
a simple channel . . .*

AN ECCLESIAL LITURGY OF REPARATION

*The Feast of the Presentation of the Blessed Virgin in the
Temple.* I saw the Most Blessed Mother radiant, escorted
by various angels and saints, who descend from heaven to
go in a great ray of light to purgatory. She had her hands
stretched out before her, as if impatient to see her children
who are in the place of expiation, and two majestic angels
opened her path: I believe one was St. Michael. When the
Blessed Virgin appeared in purgatory, there was celebration and great jubilation. The souls turned toward her,
singing, shouting praises, and entrusting intentions to her.
My guardian angel explained:

> *At times the Most High grants to some souls
> in purgatory knowledge about their relatives or
> friends who are still on earth; they become aware
> of needs or petitions that have been formulated in
> prayer. And these blessed souls then intercede for
> those relatives or friends: they direct themselves
> for this to the Immaculate Virgin, for they know
> that they find in her a powerful Queen and a
> loving Mother.*

I contemplated this bright spectacle unveiled before
my interior sight by the grace of God. The Most Holy

Virgin extended over these souls treasures of pearls, crystalline drops that emanated from her fingers and from her maternal heart, symbols of the infinite consolations that our Lord gives to the blessed souls in purgatory, dispensed by the Mother most pure. I saw the Virgin Mary as she approached this or that soul, comforting it with very sweet words, and the souls nearby, full of jubilation, rejoiced at the visit their Mother made on the occasion of her feast. They expressed gratitude for the graces and favors she obtained for all the souls in purgatory. As I watched, the Queen of Purgatory took handfuls of all kinds of consolations that looked to me like drops of dew out of two large golden chests that the angels carried. My guardian angel told me:

These are the prayers, the suffrages, the acts of virtue and piety, the yearnings of love, and the practices of charity that you do in favor of these holy souls. The Immaculate Virgin has been made the guardian of your suffrages in their favor, and she distributes these treasures unceasingly to the souls in purgatory.

See how you have to pray! Those chests must always be overflowing with your good acts, your prayers, and your yearnings of love in favor of these blessed souls.

The saints who escorted the Virgin Mary this day also came to console and to visit some souls. There were three: a pope, a martyr, and a young cleric, all with halos of light. They bent, with love and indescribably delicacy, over certain souls, consoling them and helping them to support with joy the sufferings of purgatory.[38] My angel explained it:

> These three saints have come to assist and console their children who are in purgatory—the souls of whom they are patrons, or those who had a special devotion to them. The Church celebrates their feast day today,[39] and for this occasion, they have come to visit and console the holy souls.

After this, all was erased from my internal vision, and I remained seized with an immense joy. Later, at Holy Mass, I still saw, in a great light that surrounded the celebrant and the altar, multiple souls who associated themselves

---

[38] "How can one understand the coexistence in the souls in purgatory of an unspeakable spiritual suffering—that comes from what they felt at the moment of the vision postponed by their sin—and of a joy which is also indescribable, in knowing with certainty that the battle has been won and that they will infallibly attain the divine vision? St. Thomas says that, at the level of sensibility, the sadness which contracts their heart and the joy which expands it could not exist together in a single man, but that this is possible on the spiritual level, if they refer to different things or to the same thing considered under different aspects, that they neither destroy each other nor are they incompatible. Nothing prevents, then, a man from being at the same time happy and sorrowful. When, for example, a just person is persecuted, we are at the same time happy in seeing that he is just and sad on seeing him persecuted; those two feelings do not neutralize each other, and the greater the greatness of a soul, the more his sufferings sadden us (see *Summa Theologica*, III, q. 84, a. 9 ad 2). In consequence, the coexistence of a indescribably spiritual suffering and of a joy which is also indescribable, far from being impossible, seem to be, *par excellence*, the mystery of Purgatory. St. Catherine of Genoa thought the same: 'The souls in purgatory have at the same time an excessive satisfaction and an extreme pain, without either of those two sentiments impeding one another'" (Cardinal Journet, *Le Purgatoire*, 301–302).

[39] The Pope is St. Gelasius (+496) the other two are more difficult to identify. The Church celebrated various martyrs and clergy on that day.

with the prayer and obtained numerous graces. The angel then told me:

> *My child, the blessed souls in purgatory unite themselves to the liturgy of the Holy Church, to its feasts, its celebrations, and its prayers. There is in purgatory a kind of great liturgy that is intimately united to the liturgy on earth, just as this is ordained to the heavenly liturgy. But the liturgy of purgatory is, above all, a liturgy of adoration and of reparation.*
>
> *The Queen of the Universe comes to console these holy souls on each of her feast days—above all when the Church celebrates, in joy, her Immaculate Conception and her glorious Assumption.*
>
> *Each day, the saints the Church celebrates visit purgatory to console and assist all of their children who are still suffering. Every day, the angels of the Most High come to purgatory as messengers of divine love for the holy souls.*
>
> *The greatest feast of purgatory is the commemoration of the deceased on November 2. The souls on that day receive immense consolations, and reflections of this great feast even illuminate the great purgatory.*
>
> *The entire Holy Church is united in a great prayer of intercession in favor of all the souls in purgatory, and all benefit from graces on that day, including the most abandoned and those in the great purgatory. This is the great mystery of the communion of saints.*

Toward the end of Mass, I saw numerous souls rising to celestial glory, escorted and surrounded by their guardian angels and numerous saints: it is the Most Blessed Virgin who receives them before the throne of God and, in some way, escorts them into heaven, opening the door for them. *Janua Coeli, ora pro nobis!*[40]

Among those souls is one of a priest to whom the angels give with respect a chasuble and a stole woven out of fine gold. His guardian angel also goes before him, carrying a lily in his right hand and a bouquet of red roses in the left. It is Ignatius of Loyola who first greets this priest; afterward come, resplendent from the glory of heaven, Aloysius Gonzaga and, a little further away, the apostles Peter and Paul, Pope Pius XII, and Teresa of Avila. All of them escort this priest to the Virgin Mary. She opens her arms, smiling. He, lifting up his face toward her, shows her another priest who is still in purgatory. In the end, they all enter into celestial beatitude. The priest who is still in purgatory in this antechamber of heaven approached me and told me:

> *Would you pray for me, my child? It is my brother*
> *who has gone to God with the saints for whom*
> *he had special devotion. We are two brothers*
> *who dedicated ourselves to God together. . . .*
> *He died before I did, and today we have met each*
> *other again.*

This holy priest was radiant, trembling with emotion and joy, and he spoke to me affectionately.

---

[40] Gate of Heaven, pray for us!

*How happy we are when one of us goes to heaven!
It is a little bit like an announcement of our future
liberation. And my joy is greater, since it is my
brother. . . . He will pray for me in heaven.*

What wonderful words!

I promised this priest that I would pray for him, that I would not forget him, and he told me in conclusion:

Every day there is incessant movement here. Without ceasing there are souls who arrive and others who go to heaven, above all on the great feasts of the Church and on Saturday because it is the day of Our Lady, our good Mother. All is thanksgiving here, but above all a great liturgy of reparation and expiation for the sins that we committed before . . . a great liturgy of love in communion with that of earth and that of heaven.

Afterward everything was erased from my interior gaze. My angel blessed me. I prayed, and my soul remained in a gentle peace.

IN THE UNITY OF THE MYSTICAL BODY

The Feast of the Presentation of the Virgin Mary in the Temple. After Mass, I saw fountains of twinkling stars rising from a dark pit and ascending to heaven, where they submerged themselves in an immense brightness. My angel made me understand that souls were being freed from purgatory today by the most holy Mother of God. Afterward I saw our Lady standing in a halo of light, with her right hand raised, her left hand bent toward purgatory, and the

Blood of Jesus, from his pierced Heart, extending like a river of life into her heart and from there pouring like rain from her left hand toward purgatory. I contemplated this and prayed for the souls in purgatory—in the way the saints pray for them, making them feel the attraction of the Triune God upon them.

In the glory of the saints who visit them to console them, the souls in purgatory see what they aspire to and what they are invited to, in a great power of attraction of divine love.

My angel showed me that the holy souls in purgatory have a clear intellectual vision of the perfection and sovereign goodness of God. God is a very powerful lover whom they desire (with suffering because of not possessing him now), but this desire is blocked by an obstacle—the debt they must pay for their sin. This is their torment of love, pains of desire for God which are like a terrible hunger and thirst, a torment of love scorched in total submission to the pure divine will. These holy souls, although they are hungry for God, are burning with an intense desire to satisfy the demands of his justice and to glorify his holiness. This is, in truth, an extremely painful state. The souls moan softly:

> How long will you hide your face from me,
>   O Lord?
> Free us, O God, for the glory of your name.[41]

I felt that mystical hunger of the privation of God that nothing, absolutely nothing, is capable of satisfying; it is

---

[41] See Psalms 13:1 and 79:9, *et varia.*

an ardent desire that little by little becomes stronger and more torturing, increasing both because of the memory of God—in whom one believed by faith on earth and saw in his glory at the moment of the particular judgment— and of the proximity of liberation. Along with this terrible pain, the pains of the senses, variable in form and intensity, constitute an unheard of suffering, a suffering solely of reparation and not of merit, a rigorous suffering, because purgatory is the kingdom of divine justice as well as mercy.

My guardian angel told me that the Most Blessed Virgin wants those of us here below to pray for these blessed souls as an exercise of fraternal charity. Just before the Second World War, the Most Blessed Virgin showed herself during apparitions in Heede, Germany, as Queen of the Universe and sovereign of the souls in purgatory. The angel indicated to me that these apparitions were authentic and that I should write about them since the Church has not issued any negative judgment about these events. He also told me that during these apparitions—and this is extremely significant—the Virgin Mary showed herself with the Child Jesus in her arms, since that is how she often goes to purgatory to visit the suffering souls. It is how she carries Jesus and how she gives herself to him. She is the Mother and dispenser of salvation and of light.

I saw on this occasion the Blessed Virgin descend among the souls of purgatory. They did not see the Child Jesus, but they contemplated Mary and perceived her presence, which enflamed them with a loving desire for union. The Mother of God visits purgatory every Saturday (except during Lent and Advent) and on her feast days. She obtains the liberation of numerous souls on some of these feasts, especially the Immaculate Conception, the Assumption, and the day on which the whole Church celebrates her as the Mother of God. At Christmas, too, there are many souls who, through the grace of the nativity, are admitted to the beatific vision. The Most Holy Virgin lavishes consolations and encouragement on the souls. I believe that she does not love purgatory very much and that, if she could, she would empty it with one blow: therefore, she asks us to help her with our prayers in favor of the blessed souls of purgatory.

The angel told me that these apparitions occurred in Germany and not elsewhere due to the imminent war that Germany would start. Mary attracted the attention of the people of God to purgatory so that every faithful soul could afterward recall her words and thus pray for the millions and millions of soldiers and civilians who would die in this war. In the same way, she proclaimed herself Queen of the Universe to show that she had received, by the will of God, reign over this whole world, above all the people who would later turn into fratricides, and also over heaven and purgatory.[42]

MARY IS INTERCEDING

I was able to find a little time to make my vows to the Virgin Mary, on the occasion of her feast tomorrow. In the Church, kneeling before her image at the back of the

---

[42] The apparitions took place at Heede (Germany, Osnabrück Diocese) to four young girls from November 1, 1937 to November 3, 1940. A shrine and a pilgrimage commemorate the event, which has not had any definitive judgment made on the part of the competent ecclesiastical authority.

sanctuary, I spoke to her spontaneously, like a child speaks to his mother, and this interchange suddenly filled my soul with joy. It was not a monologue, although I did not hear the voice of the Virgin Mary, nor her replies. Whoever speaks with her can be certain that she listens and even answers; she speaks to the soul without sound of words, in an infinitely gentle way, delicate and intimate. She is the Mother of fairest love.

I was occupied with this interior conversation when I saw right in front of me, in a vivid and sudden light, a surprising picture: Jesus on the cross, with long, scarlet rivers of blood pouring from his holy wounds, especially from his wounded Heart. All of this precious Blood spilled into the Sorrowful and Immaculate Heart of Mary, like an infinite and very abundant river. The Immaculate Virgin was standing before the cross with her arms lifted toward heaven in an attitude of intercession. Arrayed in light and crowned with stars, she prayed in silence with a sad and serious expression.

I saw this blood pour itself into the Heart of Mary, without a single drop being lost. From this maternal heart there sprang two great rivers—one that flowed in torrents on the earth on all humanity, and the other which fell more gently like abundant rain on purgatory. This vision caused me an immense joy, and my holy angel told me:

Mary is interceding.

Afterward I saw another image: the Most Blessed Virgin standing before the throne of God, surrounded by a cloud of fire. I did not see at that moment anything more than the splendor of the fire that hid the throne of God.

Mary elevated her right hand toward God and stretched her left hand toward earth. And from earth millions of grains of pure incense were raised up by angels, who deposited them without ceasing in the left hand of the Immaculate Virgin; she received them and put them in her heart, which seemed to me like a burning mountain of the most pure incense. This maternal heart was like a bonfire that burned without ceasing, without being consumed or decreasing, and it rose in spirals of perfumed smoke before the throne of God. All the grains of incense from earth—which are our adoration and our prayers—are carried by the angels to this maternal heart. There they burn in it and with it in the flames of the ardent and eternal bonfire of love, which is the Eucharistic Heart of Jesus, a pure bonfire of charity.

And from the throne of God poured an abundant rain of light that flowed to the right hand of Mary and from there to her Immaculate Heart. This light was then softened and became varicolored, much like the rays of sunlight are separated into multiple colors in the rainbow, and she poured this over the earth like a long, luminous river, bathing the Holy Church and falling on each soul like a sweet dew. Part of this light was directed toward purgatory, flowing in abundance on each of these holy souls like a fragrant and refreshing wave; it comforted them and alleviated much of their painful condition of purification. These are all of the graces that our Lord pours upon us through the Sorrowful and Immaculate Heart of his most holy Mother. The angel said once more:

Mary is interceding.

Finally, I saw the Most Holy Virgin seated at a table covered by an immaculate tablecloth, and she presented her heart like a splendid chalice of pure gold, full of soft nectar. She invited each soul to sit at the table and drink of this precious liquid—both the souls in purgatory and those still on earth. Afterward each soul, thus satiated, could in his or her turn bring that exquisite drink to other persons and invite them to the table. In my raptured soul I was shown that this signified the gift of unity, a gift that surges from the Eucharistic Heart of Jesus as a living fountain and is communicated to us by the Virgin Mary, Mediatrix of all graces. The angel said for a third time:

Mary is interceding.

Afterward, everything disappeared from my sight. I ended in a great celebration of acts of thanksgiving and conversation directed to our Lady, our Mother so loving.

CUSTODIAN OF THE TRUTH

On finishing my prayer, I saw Our Lady standing in an immense brilliance, with her hands raised to heaven and her heart resplendent. Waves of light that surged from this maternal heart flowed from three large rivers into purgatory, and the poor souls came there to quench their thirst and to bathe in it. I understood the symbol very well, but the souls in purgatory did something else that surprised me. They drank from one of the clear rivers and bathed in the second, obtaining all kinds of joy and consolations, but in the waters of the third river, they looked at their reflection. My guardian angel explained what I was seeing.

*These holy souls are not just looking at themselves;
they are looking at themselves in the Sorrowful
and Immaculate Heart of Mary, the image of the
holiness of God.*

*When they look at themselves in the water that
springs from her loving heart, they see themselves
as they are, still loaded down with the remains of
sin, still needing expiation.*

*These three rivers form an image: The Immac-
ulate Virgin is the custodian of the truth. The holy
souls in purgatory know this, and thus they submerge themselves in Mary the Truth, they drink of
Mary the Truth, and they contemplate the Truth in
Mary. These are the great consolations they receive
in purgatory: contemplating in Mary Immaculate
the eternal truth and receiving from Mary Immaculate the eternal truth.*

*This triple river surges from the heart of our
Queen and has its source in the Eucharistic Heart
of Jesus, who is the Eternal Truth.*

*Mary is the Mediator. You do not know this well,
but the blessed souls in purgatory—who are beggars
of love, poor, and avid for truth—know it well.*

*In the eternal heart of Mary, open upon the
whole Church, they contemplate what you very
often forget: the gift of infinite love.*

My soul marveled. I saw the Most Blessed Virgin, and
I rejoiced in seeing her—and she, with her hands elevated,
interceded for all of her children. But here below we forget the gift of our Mother. The angel concluded:

Mary gives you to Jesus.

You very often think you are very rich because you are filled with yourselves and do not pay any attention to the gift of your Mother. But the holy souls in purgatory who are very needy, who are detached from themselves, receive the gift of Jesus in Mary with an immense gratitude.

Then everything disappeared from my interior sight. While the angels sang a celestial melody, I gave thanks: Oh, Jesus, alive in Mary, save us!

TREASURER AND DISPENSER OF GRACES

Today I saw something very consoling: the Most Blessed Virgin Mary going through the world and knocking at the door of every heart. At times she is well received and is given something: flowers, candles, tears, prayers; at times—unfortunately very often—we do not want to receive her, or we are sleeping when she discretely and silently calls at our door. . . . She extends her arms to us; she opens her heart; she is overflowing with a thousand gifts of love for us, and she also receives everything we give her—which often is a wound because of our faults and weaknesses.

I have also seen Our Lady walking around, gathering into her Immaculate Heart all our gifts and offerings. Later she presents herself before the throne of the divine Trinity and shows her heart, filled with what we have given her. Then Jesus receives it, but he keeps a large part in the heart of Mary, and he adds blood and water that come forth from his divine heart. Her heart filled with the divine gifts of water and blood, Mary then goes to purgatory, where she opens her maternal heart. The blood and water deposited there by Jesus overflow like a beneficial rain. Mary adds her tears and love, and the souls receive immense relief.

Then Our Lady leaves purgatory, and her heart is filled with the gratitude and prayers of the suffering souls, which she presents to Jesus. He receives them and exchanges them for water and blood. Then the Most Blessed Virgin returns to earth, to the Church militant, and pours out the water and blood. After this she goes across the earth's surface to collect prayers, suffrages, and good works, and she presents them to her divine Son who turns them into consolations and graces for the holy souls in purgatory.

This vision brought me an enormous joy. It is just an image, certainly, but very beautiful. My guardian angel appeared to me and said:

> *See how our Queen loves you!*
> *She is the Treasurer and Dispenser of graces,*
> *the great Mediatrix of graces. Never refuse her*
> *anything. She makes of everything you do for her*
> *a treasure for the whole Church, and for you she*
> *transforms them into gifts of love.*
>
> *There is a constant transfer of love in the*
> *Church between heaven, purgatory, and earth, and*
> *the Most Blessed Virgin is actively involved in this*
> *transfer of love. The saints, including the angels,*
> *participate with her, but it is she who provides the*
> *unity, because she is the Mediatrix of love.*
>
> *You will understand these things in heaven, but*
> *you should be living them already here below.*

Then, all radiant, he disappeared in the divine light, leaving me in an act of thanksgiving.

THE SAINTS AND PURGATORY

Solemnity of All Saints—one of my favorite feast days. I contemplated the glory of God in his elect, of the mercy of God, of which we are all invited to partake. After Mass my angel approached me as I finished my thanksgiving at the altar of Our Lady, and he showed me something very beautiful. It was a castle of fire in the middle of an ocean of light. All was so resplendent that I had to look away— while my angel, on the other hand, did not stop inviting me to contemplate it. Little by little I was able to see it more easily. There was an ocean of light with two shores: one, quite somber and heavy, dark and rough, is our earth here below; the other, indescribable, radiant with light, splendor, and harmony, is heaven.

There is a constant movement between these two shores and also between both the castle of fire and the ocean of light: it is the movement of souls who, by hundreds or thousands, come each day from earth to go to heaven. A few enter immediately and many others make a stop more or less long, more or less painful, in the castle of fire, which I understood to be a symbol of purgatory. There are also angels who, also without ceasing, go in perfect harmony and diligence from heaven to earth to purgatory, and from earth to heaven to purgatory, and from purgatory to earth or to heaven. They carry all kinds of things in their arms.

The angel told me to look at heaven. There all is harmony and splendor, happiness and jubilation, an ecstasy of love around the mystery of the Holy Trinity. I saw the Holy Trinity on a throne, but it was hidden from my gaze by a cloud so brilliant that I had difficulty in looking beyond it. I saw divine love extending in luminous waves in heaven, in purgatory, and on earth; all creatures were immersed in waves of infinite love. It seemed to me that a powerful attraction of love was being exercised from the throne of the Holy Trinity. There was a strong and ardent current of love, sweet and gentle, in which all of creation, including hell, were held in some way. The saints in heaven surrender themselves without reserve to this attraction of love in a yearning of ecstasy that they continually direct toward God, who constantly gives himself to them in fullness. Thus, the saints are called to participate in this attraction of God over all of creation, to love all that God loves, and to give him glory. I feel incapable to speak of all this. . . .

After this the angel asked me to look toward the castle of fire, and I saw that all purgatory is under a powerful divine attraction of infinite love, which weighs upon it in some way. I understood that the punishment of purgatory consists in supporting with gratitude this great attraction of love, without the holy souls being able to presently correspond fully. The saints in heaven press with all the weight of their love on purgatory in this attraction of divine Love. It is the prayer of the elect for purgatory, the exercise of their love in the divine love that saturates and colors purgatory. Then I understood that the prayer and love of the saints for purgatory are different from what we feel here below for these same souls.

I saw in the midst of all the saints Mary Immaculate, their Mother and Queen. In her heart rests all the attraction of the love of God before it is poured out in waves over all creation. She receives this treasure from the Eucharistic Heart of Jesus, who pours it into her heart before it flows to all creation. All the saints surround their Mother and Queen, who is close to Jesus: This is a wonderful mystery—the saints praying and interceding in heaven united to Mary, always with her and like her, acting always with Jesus and like him as she does. Even in heaven, as Mother and Queen, Mary is the mediator of love between God and the saints.

The saints intercede in various ways for the souls in purgatory. First, they are united by love to the attraction of divine love. Then they have another means of intercession, which is love for the glory of God. They present their holiness to the divine Trinity, not as their property, but as a victory of love, a glorification of mercy. They supplicate God for this victory and glorification of Christ in them, which frees poor souls from purgatory so that they too can participate fully in the divine light.

In addition they act according to their own grace. The holy patrons show God the souls that have been entrusted to them who they have met in purgatory, who are glorified in themselves by their prayers, by their lives, by their virtues, their examples, and their imitation itself of the lives of those patrons. The saints act in this way with every soul, for every soul has its patron. Most of us realize this, but the saints also exist for the unbelievers and the faithful of other religions, for God in his infinite goodness entrusts the soul of each of his children to one or more saints who guard and protect it. The founders of religious families and the saints who have been instructed by them act in a similar way with their spiritual children and present to God all of the prayers, works, and suffrages of their congregations, asking to see these spiritual families reunited in heaven in a common glorification of God. Indeed, the saints in heaven pray to God according to the words of Jesus: "So that we may all be one."

I was shown that the elect receive, at times, suffrages from Our Lady to bring to the souls in purgatory, whom they visit to alleviate, console, enflame them with love and desire for God. I have seen that in heaven spiritual directors pray for their sons still in purgatory, and vice versa; parents pray for their children and children pray for their parents; chiefs of state for their citizens, and their people for their governors; spouses for each other who are still in the castle of fire, and friends for their friends. The bonds formed in God here below are found in God between heaven and purgatory. It is very beautiful—and surprising—because martyrs pray for their persecutors, the afflicted for their exploiters, the innocent for those who made them suffer on earth, and the poor both for those who oppressed them as well as for those who helped them, and all say:

Lord, for them we shared your cross; may we now be in your glory!

It is the great victory of love: "As we forgive those who trespass against us. . . ." Indeed, God receives the prayers of the saints to help those persons who, in one way or another, have contributed to their sanctification but are still in purgatory. In regard to this, I have been taught how powerful the prayers of the martyrs are for their executioners.

The saints help us, and they pray for those who are still on earth. But they also visit purgatory and pray for the poor souls—although without meriting for them. They invite us to pray for the souls in purgatory; they then take the suffrages they have aroused and present them to our Lord for the blessed souls that are suffering. I have seen what tenderness a holy patron has for his children in purgatory, animating those on earth to pray and offer sacrifices for them. I have also seen many times Francis of Assisi in the world inviting many men and young people with the name of Francis to pray for others of that name who are in purgatory, and other similar examples. Here I am saying things I experienced not just a few times, but hundreds of times.

In today's vision, I saw that, in heaven, the saints feel an immense joy in seeing the souls in purgatory because they know that they have been saved and are destined to be united with them and glorify God with them eternally. The saints contemplate in these souls the effects of the divine mercy, the divine victory of love and the cross. They find in these souls the virtues and charity they have loved and practiced, and they rejoice in God. God grants them many joyful motives; he sends the light of his tenderness to purgatory, often with the Most Holy Virgin, whom they escort; he sends them to meet the souls at the moment of their liberation, and he also sometimes grants the liberation of one or more souls on the day of their feast, thanks to all the suffrages of that day. The founders of religious orders have this privilege especially for their spiritual children.

I also saw some people who are already in heaven, for whom the members of their family and friends continue praying here below. They receive these prayers and suffrages from God in order to dispose of them in favor of the souls in purgatory. These saints always offer them to the Most Blessed Virgin, giving up to her in every instant the disposition of these treasures of graces, because she is their Queen and Mediator. And Mary adorns these donations with her grace, enriching them with her maternal sweetness and giving them back to these saints, asking them to apply them to such or such a soul in purgatory. In short, I was shown that, upon the beatification or canonization of a servant of God, numerous souls are liberated, especially those closest to them, their associates, and also their adversaries and even their persecutors.

All of this was shown to me with the vision of the castle of fire. My guardian angel invited me to pray without ceasing for the poor souls in purgatory, and he said to me:

The prayer and intercession of the saints for the souls in purgatory is inserted in the great call of love of heaven upon purgatory, an ardent call that the souls who are suffering feel intensely.

THE ANGELS AND PURGATORY

On this day when we pray for our dead, our Lord wanted to show my soul once more the castle of fire I saw yesterday. My holy angel, near me, told me:

Look, my child, look at the angels of God!

Then I saw the angels who, without ceasing and in constant adoration of God, go to heaven, purgatory, and earth—back and forth in a movement of a sublime harmony and perfection. These angels carry cups, flowers, and baskets in their extended hands. My heavenly guardian explained:

> *The angels are messengers of God, his emissaries all over the universe and the carriers of his light and his graces. Therefore, they are delegates among you and between the holy souls in purgatory. Haven't I been sent to you? What is my mission? To protect you, teach you, and open your soul to the marvels of the Most High and to move you to prayer, to penance, to sacrifice, and to exercise the virtues. Do you know that each time I leave you, when you do not see me near you, I am carrying to heaven a chest that you have filled with your prayers and good works, more or less according to the day. . . . And I present it at the foot of the Throne of God.*
>
> *Other angels present to the Divine Majesty the content of this basket: the grains of incense, symbol of your adoration; the roses, symbol of your good actions; pure water, symbol of your sufferings.*
>
> *The incense is burned before the Divine Majesty, who extends his great mercy over you. The roses are braided into garlands which adorn the throne of the Divine Trinity, and the pure water is collected in cups of gold. Some angels present it to Mary Immaculate, who mixes it with the unction of her maternal sweetness and commands us to extend this beneficent dew over the holy souls in purgatory.*

My soul marveled on hearing these words, and the angel showed me a multitude of spirits occupied in gathering from the surface of the earth all kinds of good works and prayers in silver baskets. Enriched with the multiple merits of the holy Church, those baskets that come from earth more or less full arrive before the throne of God overflowing with a profusion of incense, roses, and clear water.

Then I saw that other angels receive cups of nard or a similar perfume from the holy souls of purgatory. My angel showed me that these images symbolize the prayer of those souls who are suffering and their abandonment to the divine will, by which they glorify the divine Trinity. These cups come in many varied and beautiful shapes and are presented by the angels to the divine Majesty. The prayer that rises from purgatory, like all the prayer and merit that rises from earth, has a single destination: the throne of God. All converges here—every prayer and suffering of the Church militant is united to that of heaven in a common liturgy of adoration and thanksgiving. I also saw angels who go from earth to purgatory without passing (if one can say that) through heaven, and also a movement in the opposite direction. This puzzled me, but my angel explained:

The angels who go from earth to purgatory are guardian angels like myself and accompany the saved souls toward the place of their purification. This is because the particular judgment of the soul takes place in the very place of their death on earth and not in heaven, which only opens up to the souls that are perfectly purified.

As far as the angels who are going from pur-
gatory toward you, they are guardian angels who
make a trip to you and come to ask that you pray
for these holy souls and remind you of your duties
toward them, their sufferings, and their needs.
That's why you don't see anything in their hands.

Those holy spirits were not carrying anything; they
had their arms crossed over their breasts. I saw souls going
to purgatory accompanied by their guardian angels. I saw
that purgatory is surrounded by angels, and my guardian
angel told me:

They are the guardian angels of the holy souls who
are still in purgatory. They pray for them, as do
the saints, and at times they obtain from the Most
High the mission of showing themselves to these
poor souls—to console them and support them in
their hope, and to bring them a reflection of the
eternal happiness to which they are called and to
which they aspire in an ardent desire of love.

After this, my angel told me that I should look at
heaven, and upon doing so, I saw the splendor of heaven
and a throne of golden light, hidden by a resplendent
cloud. On this throne there was a palpitating, radiant
heart, appearing like gold and fire at the same time. It
was marked by a great wound in the form of a cross from
which poured forth three infinite rivers: one of crystalline
water, another of red blood, and the third of fire or light.
These rivers mixed their waves and spread them anywhere
in the whole universe without ever becoming exhausted,

enveloping and permeating all of creation and giving life to all creatures. This is the Eucharistic Heart of Jesus; my entire being shivered with joy and respect before this great mystery.

In front of this heart, outside the throne and cloud, there was another heart like a brilliant crystal, in which the river of three currents made its waters converge, pouring them into a big pond before flowing all over the universe. This is the sorrowful and Immaculate Heart of Mary. Around this heart, there was a multitude of angels in prayer, obeying a voice that came from the throne of God. They gathered garlands of roses and wove ornaments, perfumed and resplendent with freshness and colors, to adorn the heart of the Most Blessed Virgin. My angel then said to me:

> *These angels are celestial spirits whom the Most High gathers around the Immaculate to serve her, glorify her, and surround her with a radiant and deferential escort.*
>
> *They were formerly guardian angels, but the persons for whom they had charge have been condemned. . . . They are in hell forever. . . . When a sinner is lost, his guardian angel comes to increase this escort of the glories of Mary.*

Then I saw something that made a great impact upon me: Each time a guardian angels brings a basket before the throne of the Divine Majesty, another receives it and, in exchange, gives him a cup of gold and another of silver, both of them filled in the fountain of the graces that spring forth from the Eucharistic Heart of Jesus in the midst of heaven. The angel then presents these vessels to the Most Blessed Virgin who fills them a little more, while the saints also unite their offering (which is their power of intercession, greater or lesser depending on whether they have been invoked, or whether it is their feast day). The angel with the cups bows before the Most Holy Virgin, and then goes first to purgatory, over which he pours the content of the cup of gold which spreads like a refreshing, beneficial rain. Next he goes to earth, and there he gives his cup of silver (which is always filled) to a great angel who is at the side of the Holy Father—St. Michael.

St. Michael then pours the content of the cup over the holy Church, who receives all the graces and all the blessings of God and spreads and diffuses them over all mankind. Even the most intimate, most secret, most particular, and most extraordinary graces pass through our mother the Church. It is a great mystery of love. My guardian angel spoke of St. Michael with an immense respect and with great fervor:

> *Michael is our leader, the Prince of the heavenly armies. It is the Most High himself who has given him this rank over all the other angels; he is at the summit of the whole angelic hierarchy.*
>
> *He is the angel of the glory of God, and all that concerns this glory concerns him: therefore, he is also the white knight of Mary, our Immaculate Queen, the masterpiece of the glory of God. And for this reason he is the defender and protector of the Holy Catholic Church, whose mission is to give glory to God.*

He is also the angel of the judgment and of
the souls in purgatory. He is always present at
the particular judgment and assists those on their
deathbeds for the glory of God, helping them to
sustain the final combat against the dragon, who is
unchained and roars at this terrible moment.

It is also Michael who precedes our Immaculate
Queen when she visits the blessed souls in purga-
tory—and when she leads the liberated souls to
heaven, it is he who accompanies the saints to their
new home.

Do you know that Michael also always precedes
the Immaculate when she visits you here below?
He is always present at the Marian apparitions,
even though his presence may not be perceived by
anyone.

My angel stopped speaking, and I contemplated heaven
again. I saw angels who came from purgatory with cups of
nard. They gave them, as did others, to celestial spirits,
who in turn gave them a golden cup filled to the brim with
divine graces. Afterward they brought these cups to St.
Michael, who poured their content on the Holy Church.
My guardian angel said with seriousness:

These are the prayers of the holy souls in purgatory
for you who are still here on earth. If you only
knew how much those blessed souls love you! They
want you to be saved, and they want you to avoid
purgatory with its terrible sufferings, which they
know from having experienced it themselves. This

ardent desire for you is simply a loving desire to see God glorified in all things.

Pray for those blessed souls who are praying for you! Present your prayers to Our Lady, the treasurer of heaven; she will pour them like comforting and consoling dew on these holy souls who are suffering, or she will entrust them to some saints who can thus dispense them to the souls entrusted to them. No prayer is ever lost. Often there are people here below who are praying for all kinds of things, and God orders that their prayer be used in favor of the souls in purgatory—often for souls for whom those same persons have contributed to sending to purgatory by their bad example, their pernicious influence, their straying, their unconsidered words. This is a form of reparation that God, exercising his justice, concedes to some souls in purgatory.

Then the angel showed me something else. Some souls that come from here below and enter into purgatory emerge immediately and rise, radiant, to heaven. I wondered at this, and my angel explained joyfully:

These holy souls who scarcely pass through purgatory we call "lightning souls." We have just enough time to see them go through purgatory. They launch themselves rapidly into the fire in order to submerge themselves quickly in the purification. Then they enter almost immediately into the heavenly Jerusalem.

If you only knew what purgatory is like!

While I finished saying the Rosary for the souls in purgatory, my guardian angel showed himself to me, kneeling to say the Glory Be to the Father with me. Upon rising, he put his hands on the cross that adorned his tunic and said very seriously:

Continue praying like this, and get those around you to pray for those poor holy souls who are suffering. You don't know what purgatory is like, nor how much the poor souls there have to endure[43] and how many of them are abandoned . . .

If the whole world knew what purgatory was like, it would be emptied in a short time as a result of prayers and mortifications—and how your lives would change! But there are many among you who cover their faces; they do not want to take the time to ask God to explain this great mystery to them or fill them with compassion for these poor souls. Purgatory is not a myth; it is a reality that many have to experience. Wanting to negate its existence, one runs the risk of spending a lot of time there,

---

[43] St. Veronica Giuliani (+1727), in her office of "helper of the souls in purgatory," experienced in a mysterious and surprising way the pain of privation of God that the souls suffer: "It is the pain of pains," she wrote; "the privation of God did not last more than an instant, and [yet] it would be capable of annihilating us. Knowing by an interior light that we are lacking the Supreme Good is the supreme evil. Fire, ice, sharp instruments, and all the punishments that one could imagine: What are they compared to this pain? If a soul were to return to earth, he would be incapable of describing it, just as St. Paul could not describe heaven when he returned from there. But how can I be quiet! I will call it the nothing" (St. Veronica Giuliani, *Le Journal* [*Diario* in the Italian], [Gembloux: Duculot, 1931]).

including the risk of being lost for all eternity. And contemplating it only through one's imagination, one has a great possibility of experiencing it cruelly.

These words made me tremble. The angel was silent and looked at me with an impressive gravity, his arms crossed, resplendent with a vivid light. I prayed with him. Afterward I asked him what Jesus wanted of me in this regard—poor, miserable me! The angel separated his hands very slowly, which were partly hiding the cross, and he showed it to me with his right hand, while with his left he pointed to his purple belt and said:

You know it: pray, do penance, sanctify yourself in silence and in the fulfillment of the duties of your state, and offer everything for the holy souls. You should also ask your neighbors and friends to pray for the souls in purgatory, and ask the priests that you know to preach on this mystery, which is so often forgotten.

Really, you don't know what purgatory is like; if you knew, you would work very seriously for your eternal salvation, and you would try with your prayers to obtain the freedom of these souls who are suffering so much.

After saying these words, the angel crossed his arms again and then disappeared.

ACCELERATE BY LOVE, THE HOUR OF ENCOUNTER

When I finished my prayer, my guardian angel presented himself to my interior sight and said gravely:

The time that is given to you on earth should serve
to prepare you for your encounter with God.
    If you really understood this, purgatory would
not exist, because souls would do all that was pos-
sible to be ready for the moment of encounter.

But God, knowing our weakness, created it, because
he wants to save us. . . . Responding to this idea I was
formulating, my angel continued:

Purgatory was created by God. It is a masterpiece
of his infinite mercy. But if souls really made an
effort, this extra grace would not be necessary and
purgatory would disappear for lack of use. It is
souls who maintain the need for purgatory, because
they are not prepared at the moment of their
encounter. If you reach the end of your life cleansed
of all sin and having paid on earth the debt of sin,
purgatory would then not exist, because you would
go directly to heaven.

God knows us, and he knows well, unfortunately, that
there will always be poor sinners on earth. . . . The angel
began to speak again:

You should make an effort to do all you can to
avoid purgatory and go directly to heaven after
your death.
    If you knew what purgatory was like, you
would do everything to avoid it and would take
advantage of the time granted you on earth to
advance, through love, the hour of your meeting
with God.

I asked him then to let me know what we have to do to advance that hour of meeting with God, so that we can avoid purgatory after our death. He explained to me:

You have to surrender yourself totally to divine love. You have to let yourself be transformed by love until you are converted into a perfect instrument of love.

Do you know how to achieve this? Give yourself in everything to the pure will of God. Make an effort to fulfill the demands of this pure will, which is love. This is the perfection that is asked of you, and you should work for one thing only: to glorify God, who is love. The glory of the divine Trinity should be your only preoccupation, and you should unify your whole life in love for this.

Your whole life should be directed to divine love and oriented in its smallest aspects toward the glory of God: for this you have to pray more than speak, act in charity more than making speeches, and be rooted in silence and humility to make your faith and hope grow. Look only at God—and at God in others—to attain forgetfulness of self and thus acquire the grace of doing everything in the light of faith, the dynamism of charity, and the measure of hope.

Do you know what is one of the greatest errors some souls make?

They want to avoid purgatory at all costs, and they try, sometimes recklessly, to do everything to go directly to heaven. But they are motivated by fear and not stimulated by love. They are acting more for themselves than seeking only the glory of God.[44]

Understand well what I am telling you now: The only way to avoid purgatory is not to do everything to avoid it, but to do everything to go to heaven.[45] *It is to work untiringly for your own perfection and salvation, giving yourself fully to the infinite love of God in conformity in everything with his demands, not having anything else in mind other than the glory of God. Everything else is vanity.*

All of this was severe, austere, and at times difficult to understand. I asked my guardian angel to explain in particular what he meant by this expression, to act "in the measure of hope," and he offered the following commentary:

A soul who acts in the measure of hope is a soul for whom hope has only one objective: God.

Hope is a humble and confident waiting for the eternal possession of God. Hope is measured when

---

[44] See St. Thérèse of Lisieux: "I would not have wanted to pick up a piece of straw to avoid purgatory. Everything that I did was to please God, and for him, to save souls" (*Novissima Verba*).

[45] "You are not trusting enough," said St. Thérèse of the Child Jesus to a fearful sister. "You have too much fear of God, and I can assure you that this is an affliction. Do not fear purgatory because of the pain that they suffer there, but desire not to go there to please God, who dislikes so much to impose this expiation on people. Seek to please him in everything; if you have an unbreakable trust that he will purify you at every instant in his love, and will not leave on you a single stain of sin, you can be well sure that you will not go to purgatory" (Fr. Philip of the Trinity, *La doctrine de Sainte Thérèse de l'Enfant-Jésus sur le Purgatoire* [Librairie du Carmel, 1950], 11–12).

*it is exercised truthfully and effectively in a simple
and serene way. It detaches the soul from earthly
goods and from all vain pleasures and satisfactions.
It also arouses in the soul great desires for holiness;
it opens itself in filial trust toward God throughout
one's earthly life and in final perseverance at the
hour of one's death.*

*But there are souls who imagine that they are
practicing hope while they are sunk in presumption
or lose themselves in useless dreams, giving free rein
to their imagination, especially in what concerns
their final goals.*

I received this teaching with joy and peace, and my
soul was grateful to God for so many graces. After explaining this to me, my angel continued:[46]

*When you evoke the final end, you very often
waste your time in sterile discussions, in risky*

---

[46] How long does purgatory last? Soto taught that the wait for eternal happiness should not surpass a certain number of years; Bede and Denys of Chartreux, that it could be prolonged to the end of time; St. Bonaventure believed that in purgatory there were punishments less than the greatest pains on earth; St. Augustine, that the greatest pains of this life did not equal the smallest pains of the other world.

What do we have to believe? Nothing more than what the Church teaches, which is the doctrine that cements our faith. The Church affirms that "the sinner must suffer temporal punishment in this life or in the other to obtain the full remission of his sins and enter into the kingdom of heaven; that purgatory exists and that souls who are detained there are helped by the suffrages of the faithful and, above all, by the precious Sacrifice of the Altar" (Jacques Monsabre, *Exposition du Dogme Catholique*, Lent of 1889 [Paris: Lethielleux, 1901], 221). Only; let us always remember the revelation that Our Lady made to the children of Fatima: a young friend, Amelia, "would be in purgatory until the end of the world" (apparition of May 13, 1917).

speculations, or in narrow and false reasoning: vain chattering!

There is need for great discretion on this subject. One often gives too much importance to the imagination, which does not allow us to see heaven, purgatory, and hell as one might look on a stage in a theater.

You cannot know what purgatory is; it is better to remain for a longer time on earth and suffer the worst evils with love and resignation than be in purgatory for one hour. An hour in purgatory is terrible—it is longer than a year with great sufferings on earth, and the most atrocious sufferings in your life on earth are a soothing balm in comparison with what the poor and holy souls in purgatory are enduring.

Yes, the sufferings of purgatory are incomparably worse than the most you can suffer on earth, but one cannot compare them because they belong to two different orders. And think that most of the souls have to remain thirty or forty years in purgatory.

Do you understand how much you have to pray for them?

The angel became silent and then disappeared from my interior sight.

PART

3

"I was in prison
and you visited me."

—Matthew 25:36

"Behold,
I spent the night praying
for the souls in purgatory,
and the day for the conversion of sinners.
The practice of prayer
for liberation from purgatory is,
after having prayed for the conversion
    of sinners,
the most pleasing to God."

—The Holy Curé of Ars

Don't be curious

These are words directed to me by a soul in purgatory after relaying the substantial information God permitted him to offer me about purgatory. This soul was expiating his grave faults there for a long time, and he showed himself to me on various occasions so that I would pray and ask others to pray for his liberation. This is what he told me:

> Never try to scrutinize the plan of divine justice! Many people ask questions about the number of those chosen, and this causes them to take the path of error.
>
> The judgment of God is never comparable to that of men, and many will be surprised at the day of final judgment. They will see souls saved that a false idea of divine justice would have condemned to perdition, and others condemned who sometimes were taken for saints.
>
> Do not be curious! Pray for us, who have such need of your charitable aid, of all your good actions, all of your suffrages. Learn this well and make it a strict rule for yourself: By the infinite mercy of God, there are certainly many more souls saved than condemned. But one always has to pray for the deceased, however

*brilliant their reputation for piety or sanctity may
have been.*

*The only thing that we can be sure of is that a soul
that has been beatified is in heaven.*

*For all of the other souls, including those
known as "servants of God," there is no general
rule. Many are sadly still in purgatory, for no one
laughs at God's justice!*

*So as long as God allows you, never stop pray-
ing for those souls whose process of beatification is
open: some of them are with us, and those prayers
help them and console them.*

Praised be Jesus Christ, our gentle Savior!

The soul disappeared after this invocation. I remained
somewhat saddened, but I recovered quickly, meditating on what I had been told. In all these questions, the
really important thing is to pray with confidence, without seeking to know more things, or worse yet, to imagine them.

During that same day, I saw a great number of souls
who were entering eternity—many, unfortunately, who
were falling into the abyss of eternal condemnation! I will
not say anything about this, because the terrible mystery of
the inferno belongs to the secrets of God. All those souls
entering eternity were like a heavy rain (there were millions), and among them I saw only one enter directly into
heaven. He was a resplendent little child who must have
died at two or three years of age. His guardian angel carried him in his arms, raising him with himself to paradise,

leaving in the dark sky a long trail of iridescent light. There are thousands of souls of children who, in spite of their few years of life, have had to skim briefly through purgatory. They are only briefly there, but they have to go through this . . . and many babies who go like little angels toward limbo.[1]

Among the souls that go to purgatory, I have seen people of every age and walk of life: children (five years old or a little older), adults, adolescents, the elderly, etc. I have seen priests, religious, monks, politicians, workers, artists, the poor, the wealthy—people from all walks of life. There were members of my own family and also all kinds of people I knew in other times, which caused me both a vivid sorrow and a profound relief. . . . The judgments of God are unfathomable, and one often makes the mistake of wanting to rashly judge the eternal fate of persons that one has known well. The judgments of God are not comparable to ours. He judges in his infinite wisdom and we according to our human vision, which is often so limited.

He also showed me that officially canonized saints have gone through purgatory, and I had the joy of knowing of others who went directly to heaven. These are much fewer than those who go to purgatory. They are really mistaken

---

[1] St. Teresa of Avila states in her autobiography that among the many souls whose fate had been revealed to her, only three had avoided going to purgatory (*Autobiography*, ch. 38). And the Holy Curé of Ars did not hesitate to affirm in a sermon: "It is certain that very few of the elect have not passed through purgatory, and that the pains that they suffer there are greater than anything that we can understand" (*Sermons*, vol. 4 [Paris: Beauchesne, 1909], 178).

who imagine that the mercy of God might be united to a kind of sentimental paternalism that would find excuses and justifications for everything. Oh no, this is not the case! Pray, pray, pray . . .

O Lord, enlighten my soul
and guide me into your will!
O Mary, teach me to glorify
the Divine Trinity!

People of every age and condition

I had the grace of being able to dedicate some time during the morning to pray for the souls in purgatory. I was finishing the Rosary when I saw a vivid light. My guardian angel, who was close to me, took holy water and gave it to me. I sprinkled it over that strange light; it opened up and I understood that it was purgatory. I saw a place without limits or borders, only the cross. I saw millions of souls sunk in the pain of the fire of divine love. It was like a furnace where only the river of blood of the Immaculate Lamb could ease the flames, bringing consolation to the souls. My angel told me:

Offering Masses for them is what provides the
greatest alleviation to the souls in purgatory.[2]
This is why during the Holy Mass you remember
the dead, underlining the unity of the complete

---

[2] The principal means of helping the deceased is the Holy Sacrifice of the Mass, because it continues the offering of Christ on the cross and has, so to speak, an infinite satisfactory value; after this are prayer, alms, and the common suffrages of the Church.

Mystical Body and calling on you for prayer for
their intentions, which is a duty for the celebrant
and also for the faithful.

The holy souls in purgatory have a right to your
prayer, both liturgical and personal prayer. This has
been established by the Most High.

I was facing millions of souls. There were people of
every condition, nation, and epoch, people of all ages. I
saw the great of this world and the humble (humble in the
sense of their social condition, for there are no spiritually
humble people in purgatory). There were children and old
people, husbands and wives, both men and women religious, adolescents, kings, farmers, workers, poor and rich,
and also bishops, popes, officials, professors, etc. This
vision caused me some fear, but also an unprecedented
amazement; above all it inflamed in me the desire to pray
for these souls. I understood that our Lord wanted me to
record these visions for this end: so that we would pray for
these holy souls to speed up their liberation. Then everything was erased.

SOULS EXTENDING THEIR HANDS

The Holy Mass is the fountain of all graces, and during the
entire day I felt internally a gentle light that opened the
eyes of my soul to the invisible realities of the supernatural world. From where I was, I saw multitudes of souls in
purgatory: They came in silence, and most of them were
covered with a kind of ashy mist. The were extending their
hands, as if begging for more prayers. What emotional

symbolism! I offered for them all that I had done during the day.[3]

During the Way of the Cross (which I dedicated especially to the souls in purgatory), these souls were behind me, and I saw a haze of small drops of dew that blossomed from my prayer and fell over them like a refreshing light rain. I invoked our Lord and asked him to renew upon these souls the abundant and vivifying effusion of his most precious Blood; at various times I saw how a double tide of blood came forth from the wounds and the burning Heart of Jesus crucified—or rather, that all of his blood reunited in a single river to pour itself out in two burning waves. The first irrigated the Church militant on earth, and the other rested like a cloud over purgatory. When I presented this redemptive Blood to the Father, a ray of light fell upon the holy souls of purgatory, who received it like a beneficial rain. They were like people dry and lost in the desert who suddenly receive a plentiful rain of clear, fresh water.

---

[3] The faithful can help the souls in purgatory function in the bond of charity that unites the members of the Church. The efficacy of this help is based on the mystery of the communion of saints: the union in charity makes all goods common to all: "All of the faithful united by charity do not form more than a single body which is the Church. But in a single body, the members help one another" (St. Thomas Aquinas, *Summa Theologica*, Supplement, q. 71, a. 1). The suffrages cannot change the state of the deceased person, but they contribute to reducing his pain and advancing the time of his liberation. For a good work done by a living person to be useful for the dead, they have to be united to each other by the bond of charity; and the good work carried out has to be done for the intention of the deceased. This intention for the deceased can be considered as having been done by him or her. The suffrages are presented to the divine mercy. They are presented to God for the deceased, either as merit—its efficacy then rests on a decision of divine justice—or as prayer—its efficacy then depending on the divine liberality.

At the end of the evening, I entered a church, took some holy water and sprinkled it on the stones, following the custom of other countries, and said to our Lord: "My God, a little holy water for the suffering souls." And there came a light spring, which mitigated the thirst of a multitude of souls in purgatory. All of this came about in silence, within a great peace. I understood that offering all we do in a day can serve as a suffrage: prayers, good works, acts of piety and devotion, aspirations to our Lord, the Blessed Virgin, and the saints, acts of humility, all sufferings, little voluntary mortifications, resignation in sickness and in the face of death—in summary, all that we are able to do. And when we are praying for a special intention, we can associate the holy souls in purgatory with it. This will not take efficacy from our special intention; on the contrary, it will be enriched in that way.

The souls in purgatory don't monopolize anything; instead, they enrich our prayers. Our prayer, then, has a great ecclesial dimension, from earth to heaven. In giving thanks to God for making me understand this, I contemplated these things that gave me great light and brought me peace.

THE DURATION AND INTENSITY OF PURGATORY

On finishing the prayer, I saw a great light, and a person appeared who had several times come to ask me for prayers. Radiantly, he extended his hands to me, saying:

Ah, my child! Thank you for your prayers, for the Holy Masses offered for my intention, and above all, for the visits to the sick. You acquired many

merits for me, and this has been a great relief. Now
I am going to heaven!

My soul was delighted by this visit and his consoling words. I told this to the person, who continued speaking:

I was in purgatory for thirteen years—thirteen
years burning with desire for God in this purifying
light of the antechamber of paradise. And now I am
going to my Savior!

I answered that soul that he had been there for a long time and that we could not imagine it. The soul answered with a smile:

Oh no, that is neither short nor long. It was just
the right amount of time: You cannot understand
this, but here in purgatory the time and the inten-
sity of one's pains form a single thing.
    Our greatest suffering is our nostalgia for God.
The more we wait for someone we love, the more
slowly the time passes, and the greater is our suffer-
ing in this waiting.
    This is a little bit of what purgatory is!

As he spoke, I saw a great, radiant brightness open up over him. Angels dressed in white and crowned with red roses appeared, preceding the Most Blessed Virgin, St. Francis of Assisi (whose wounds were like burning suns), and two holy friends of this soul: Teresa of Avila and Thérèse of Liseux. The soul sighed, and a powerful impulse carried him toward the Virgin Mary, who opened her arms. I saw him kneeling at the feet of Our

Immaculate Mother, and then he turned toward me and spoke once again:

> *I am going to tell you what purgatory is.*
> *It is the configuration of the soul to its true dimension for eternity—its full dimension in Jesus, crucified and glorified, a dimension measured by love and inaugurated in baptism.*
> *This configuration is completed in purgatory during a long and painful purification. I give thanks to all who prayed for me. I will not forget you in heaven.*

And as everything disappeared from my interior sight, I remained in the jubilation of thanksgiving.

THE JOYS OF PURGATORY

Morning prayer. A great light appeared before my interior vision, and I contemplated an elderly nun who had a golden sieve filled with burning coals in her hand. She came toward me and said, "Praised be Jesus Christ forever!" I saw that it was a holy soul from purgatory. She asked me:

> *My child, would you like to pray for me? No one prays for me because I died in great peace with a reputation for holiness. My dear sisters surely believe I am in paradise, and thus they don't pray for me.*

I promised to pray for her, and she became radiant; an intense light saturated her with its rays. She continued:

*As you can see, I am in the antechamber of par-
adise, languishing from love, close to my divine
Spouse; this love is both the cause of my joy and
the pain that tortures me. Pain is our joy in purgatory, because it is a torment of love, a sickness
of love.*

I prayed for this soul, and from time to time some red
embers fell from her sieve, which emptied itself little by
little, but the nun did not notice. Overjoyed and lifting her
eyes to heaven, she said to me:

*You have begun to know purgatory, yet you have
not experienced either its joys or its pains.*

*Tell your brethren that your greatest joys on
earth are nothing more than wind and smoke
compared to the sublime joys of purgatory. The
greatest happiness for a soul is to be in heaven. It
is eternal bliss! But immediately after this, there is
no joy greater than to savor the joys of purgatory.
And know this: The more our union goes toward
plenitude, the more our pains diminish; they are
concentrated until they disappear. Nothing remains
except this sickness of love that we know in the
antechamber of paradise.*

*Yes, speak of the pains of purgatory, but speak
also of its ineffable joys!*

Radiant, she disappeared from my interior sight, leaving me greatly consoled.

THE SOULS IN PURGATORY LOVE US

During the day I dedicated some moments to praying for the souls in purgatory, and I received comforting consolations. When I finished praying the Stations of the Cross, my guardian angel appeared to me, saying:

> *This is good, my child. One has to pray for these holy souls. Seek even the smallest moment of the day to offer sacrifices to God for them. To pray for them is a debt of charity that glorifies the Almighty, and it is also a debt of recognition for you.*

This last word surprised me, and I asked my angel to explain it. He continued gravely:

> *Yes, it is a duty of recognition. The holy souls in purgatory are praying for you, interceding for you before the divine majesty, within the limits that God assigns them. Their prayers and their protection are very powerful for the Church militant.*

This caused me great joy, and I continued listening to the angel.

> *The souls in purgatory are not considering themselves. They have only one thirst, which is to glorify God.*
> *At times the divine mercy shows them souls on earth: their aspirations, their trials, and their works; but above all, God's design for them. Then the souls pray that this design be fulfilled. They love you perfectly in God, because they are not absorbed in their pain nor inhibited by their*

sufferings. They are not fixed on themselves, so they look at you in God, and for God, praying for you in the divine light.

They are not conscious of your purely human qualities, which have no value in purgatory and won't have any value in heaven either. Your only treasure is the exercise of virtue, faithful prayer, and the treasures of grace that our Holy Mother the Church puts at your disposal. All the rest is no more than vanity, destined to be burned in the fire of charity that should be burning in you.

My soul savored this lesson the angel had dispensed to me with gravity and sadness in his voice. I asked him the reason for this.

It's because you don't love God enough, because you do not work enough for his glory! And the souls in purgatory see this when God shows it to them, and for them this is another cause for suffering. And this causes them to multiply their prayers for those close to them who are still on earth, their benefactors, and all the souls our Lord indicates to them.

They pray also for all the intentions they neglected when they were on earth. But, as I have explained to you, they never pray for themselves.

Within the limits assigned to me by obedience to my spiritual father, I could ask my angel in what form these souls know us.

*I have already told you, my child: in the light
of divine mercy. Their way of knowing is more
elevated than yours on earth. It is comparable to
our own. These souls have an intuitive knowledge
of the Church militant and of its needs insofar
as our Lord permits it, for this knowledge is only
exercised within the providential limits assigned
by God.*

*At times he reveals to these souls your prayers,
needs, and sufferings. Then they intercede and pray
for you, and they obtain for you protection of a
spiritual and temporal kind. At other times, our
Lord allows them to show themselves to incite you
to pray for them, to revive your fervor and your
love, or to protect you from danger. This situation
is not frequent, but it happens because our Lord
permits it. All of this is shown to you when you
love these souls. You should pray for them, do good
works, and make sacrifices in their favor, to alleviate their pain.*

*A person who really wants to help these souls
will go to Mass every day and pray especially for
them, especially in the Memento of the Dead,[4] and
he or she will pray the Rosary every day with some
intention for these blessed souls and will also make
the Stations of the Cross for the great intentions of
the Church and for these blessed souls.*

---

[4] "The sacrament of the Eucharist frees man from purgatory, given that it is
a sacrifice of satisfaction for sin" (St. Thomas Aquinas, *Summa Theologica*,
IIIa q. 52, a. 8, ad 2).

These are the three great means of alleviating them: Holy Mass, the Rosary, and the Stations of the Cross. The Blood of Jesus Christ is a great consolation for them. And the Mother of God sends true fountains of consolation to the souls in purgatory.

The angel left, and I remained in great joy and serenity.

CREATED BY MERCIFUL LOVE

This day I offered Holy Mass especially for the soul of a young priest whom I had the grace of assisting during his agony and death. During the thanksgiving, my soul enjoyed the splendor of divine light, and I saw with the eyes of my spirit the young priest rising into heaven, accompanied by a group of saints: St. Francis of Paola, St. Rita of Cassia, and St. Gabriel of the Sorrowful Virgin. Perhaps these were saints to whom he had particular devotion. This glorious cortege rose up to Mary, the Holy Mother of God, who was dressed in white, with her arms outstretched toward him. I believe that the Most Blessed Virgin was there to receive this son and introduce him to the presence of the Divine Trinity. It was so beautiful!

When the priest reached the Mother of God, she smiled with tenderness and pointed to me with a gesture of her hand. Then the priest turned toward me, extended his hands, and said with a smile:

Thank you! Thank you for your prayers and your help . . .
I am going to the house of the Father, but know that I won't forget you!

Tell everyone that purgatory was created by merciful love and is the masterpiece of divine mercy and of divine justice.

Just one of our sins would merit eternal fire, but the Father does not want his sons to die; he wants their health and their life in him forever. . . . Tell all your brothers that purgatory was created by divine mercy.

My soul was enraptured. The priest traced a great cross of light over me and entered into eternal glory with the Most Holy Virgin. Then everything was blotted from my interior sight.

THE PARTICULAR JUDGMENT

I was watching at the side of a dying person, in silence and prayer. Words seemed vain in the presence of the mystery of a person who had lost consciousness and was at the point of his transition to the next life. On this occasion, our Lord gave me light about the particular judgment of a soul.[5] My guardian angel was visible to my soul, sustaining and guiding me. As soon as the person died—it was an adolescent—I saw his soul gently abandon his body. I understood then why the body is called *remains*. Immediately

---

[5] "By faith we believe that death is followed immediately by the particular judgment, in which God awards eternal retribution to each one in accord with his or her works" (Councils of Florence and Trent). The *Catechism of the Catholic Church* declares: "Each man receives his eternal retribution in his immortal soul at the very moment of his death, in a particular judgment that refers his life to Christ: either entrance into the blessedness of heaven—through a purification or immediately—or immediate and everlasting damnation" (1022).

the soul found itself in the presence of a resplendent and blinding light. My angel told me at that moment:

The resplendent light is the glory of God; it is the splendor of his holiness. From the instant the soul separates from the body, it is in the presence of the glory of God. It does not see God, but it does see the splendor of his holiness.[6]

I was then able to understand a number of operations that took place successively, and at the same time, beyond any consideration of time and space. In the first place, I saw the soul transfixed by the beams of the bright light that invaded it. All its sins and bad inclinations had

---

[6] At the moment of appearing before God, souls have defective dispositions, as they usually refer to the remains of sin, due to the consequences of original sin and of actual sin. According to St. Thomas Aquinas, even the holiest saints, at the end of their pilgrimage on earth, suffer "the disordered fruit of original sin." In what do these defective dispositions consist? Can one say, as this account of purgatory indicates, that they disappear in the burning light of the particular judgment? Original sin, blotted out by baptismal grace, leaves nevertheless a disorder in the faculties of the soul, an effect of the loss of original justice. Because of this disorder, man has difficulty in elevating himself toward God and submitting to him. The natural inclination toward a good act is as if wounded, while the interior powers of sensibility and imagination escape in some way from the control of the spiritual soul, exercising over the soul a tyranny which made St. Paul say that he did the evil that he did not want to do, and did not do the good that he wished to do. This disorder of interior powers of the soul and the body constitute what theologians usually call the *home of greed* (or concupiscence), which on earth the sacraments combat effectively, without causing that "state of concupiscence" to disappear. At death, the divine light causes it to disappear completely from the soul in the state of grace.

In this movement of attraction and light of the truth, the soul finds itself comforted in a personal way, by God himself. Without showing himself to the soul, he shows himself in light, by the attraction of love.

disappeared (I believe with death itself). There did not remain in this soul anything more than the punishment for sins committed and not expiated. Even bad inclinations toward evil had been straightened out, as though they had been dissolved under the traces of that extraordinary light. It's very difficult to explain this. It seems to me that getting used to sin leaves in us a kind of debility, leaving us vulnerable to evil. All of this is what had disappeared.

At the same time, in the presence of the glory of God, the soul remains radically absorbed in love. It submits to a prodigious attraction and responds by surrendering itself in the full exercise of its will to the pure will of God. Through the rays of light, the soul perceives that the holiness of God has pierced it, inflaming it with love. It is as if the soul feels a divine light of truth at the very instant it gives in to a violent horror of sin and its consequences. The soul knows this hatred of sin because it is immersed in the divine light, which shows it the infinite perfection of the love of God.[7]

---

[7] After death, in the divine light, the soul sees clearly the venial sins for which he or she did not have effective contrition on earth. The soul immediately repents and thus obtains divine forgiveness. Since this repentance comes after death, it is no longer meritorious; the soul does not benefit any more either in its growth in charity or its remission of punishment. The Church has not made a pronouncement on this delicate matter, much debated by theologians. We will not give here the history of their discussions. It is enough to recall that St. Thomas Aquinas appears to have changed his opinion during the course of his life. In his commentary on the sentences, a work of his youth, he declared, in effect: "Venial sin is remitted in the next world, by the fire of purgatory." On this debated question, Aquinas's *De Malo* affirmed, on the contrary, that venial sin is remitted before entry into purgatory.

In this movement of attraction and light of truth, the soul finds itself comforted in a personal way by God himself. Without showing himself to the soul, he manifests himself by the attraction of love. It is an unexpected but intensely desired encounter. In responding to so much solicitude by divine love, the soul discovers in itself a grievous obstacle, very painful, that prevents it from surrendering itself totally to the loving attraction of God. This is the penalty of the sinner: that which remains to be expiated to satisfy the justice of God. I saw this soul in this state of being torn, which constitutes the essential mystery of purgatory: the tearing of the soul between its attraction to the love of God and its incapacity to respond to it.[8]

All this was clear to my mind, but I cannot express it clearly, because words are powerless to describe these things. At the same time, I saw with the eyes of my soul a series of images.

I saw the guardian angel of the adolescent praying at his side and also the Blessed Virgin, who prayed standing in the glory of God, together with other saints. They were all interceding for this soul. Very much below, I contemplated a fiery black abyss, where the devil was unchained, roaring, vomiting, and screaming with hellish anger, undoubtedly because this saved soul had escaped from him. . . .[9]

---

[8] See St. Catherine of Genoa, *Treatise on Purgatory*, II.

[9] "O Lord Jesus Christ, King of glory, deliver the souls of all the faithful departed from the pains of hell and from the bottomless pit: deliver them from the lion's mouth, that hell swallow them not up, that they fall not into darkness, but let the standard-bearer Holy Michael lead them into that holy light" (liturgical prayer).

I don't know whether the soul was able to see all of this; to me this was shown as a personal act of God in the soul, an internal confrontation of the soul with the mystery of God. I think that, in those moments, the soul has no vision other than the glory of God. I believe, however, that he senses all of this and knows more than what he sees. The intercession of the Most Holy Virgin really exists, and she exercises it with power. The saints also intercede, although at the moment of judgment the soul does not see or have more than an intuitive knowledge. This intercession seems very strong to me, and all of heaven participates in it. It is a formidable impulse of general love for each soul that arrives before God.

I did not hear God formulate a sentence. The judgment is pronounced, but in the secret of the intimate relationship of God with the soul appearing before him. I believe that this is the consequence of the knowledge the soul receives in this light of truth, and this sentence—if one can call it that—is perceived immediately by the soul confronted with the splendor of the divine holiness. The soul itself conforms to the will of God, which is love and justice. For the soul, this conformity is the occasion to exercise its freedom fully, which is a gift of divine love. It surrenders to it, according to its proper state—that is, entering into the glory of heaven, withdrawing to purgatory, or hurling itself into the fire of hell.

One can never know fully the falseness of representing God as a terrifying being who, with an accusing finger, points to purgatory or hell. No: God is love, and love attracts all to himself. The eternal destiny of a soul is not a decision of God. It is a free decision of the soul![10]

The soul of the adolescent that I saw in the presence of the glory of God withdrew calmly to purgatory, remaining in the vivid attraction of divine love. In purgatory souls seemed to continue to perceive the splendor of the holiness of God and experience impetuously the attraction and power of his love.

The particular judgment develops in a single act; it is a gift of the love of God for the soul. After the judgment (which is outside of time as we understand it), the soul enters into greater and more elevated knowledge, although the merits it acquired on earth do not increase at all, nor its glory in heaven. But the more God purifies it in the fire of his holiness, the more it rises toward him. And if the soul is admitted to the beatific vision, it receives knowledge immediately.

---

[10] St. Thérèse of the Child Jesus wrote to Fr. Roulland: "I know that one has to be good and pure to appear before God, but I also know that our Lord is infinitely just, and this justice, which frightens so many souls, is the subject of my joy and my confidence. To be just is not only to exercise severity to punish the guilty; it is also to recognize right intentions and reward virtue. I hope both in the justice of God and in his mercy, because he is compassionate, full of gentleness, slow to punish, and abundant in pity. He knows our fragility and recalls that we are no more than dust. As a father has tenderness toward his children, thus our Lord has compassion on us" (S. 102, 8. 14. 13). And later she added: "When I read certain spiritual writings, where perfection is shown through a thousand hardships, surrounded by a multitude of illusions, my poor spirit is quickly fatigued; I close the wise book because my head is breaking, my heart drying up, and I go to Holy Scripture. Then everything appears bright to me: a single word opens up infinite horizons to my soul; perfection seems easy to me. I see that it is enough to recognize our nothingness and abandon ourselves like a child in the arms of God" (*Letters*, Central Office of Lisieux, pp. 392–394).

When a soul is admitted to the beatific vision, it receives immediately knowledge of God himself, to whom it remains united, and in the knowledge of God it receives also knowledge of the mysteries of heaven.

In purgatory, the soul at times receives a visit from its guardian angel, the Blessed Virgin, and some saints (especially on their liturgical feasts). It sees them in God and contemplates them in him, who still remains hidden. Insofar as hell is concerned, the soul is submitted by its state to the perception of demons, the condemned, the spirits of darkness, and the diabolical world. Our Lord showed all this to me on the occasion of the death of my adolescent friend.

LIGHT ON THE STATE OF THE SOULS IN PURGATORY

When I was making a holy hour for the souls in purgatory, I understood that we can alleviate the sufferings of these souls and shorten the time of their purification by our prayers and sacrifices. The Mass especially is of inestimable value when it is offered for that intention, especially when heard with recollection during the week. Works of charity—visiting the sick, almsgiving, and welcoming one's neighbor—also have great value. God converts our efforts and good will into graces for these holy souls, who are very grateful to us.

The souls who suffer most in purgatory are those who sinned against charity, those who, in the course of their life on earth, did not become more perfect in this virtue and did not know how to be detached from themselves and give themselves to God and their neighbor. I saw how sins of the tongue, avarice, envy, and attachment to material goods are the cause of particularly severe punishment in purgatory. By contrast, charity, mercy, patience, gentleness, humility, and joy communicated to others, along with abandonment to the will of God (above all when death is approaching), are attitudes that can shorten time in purgatory.

From the time that, by God's will, a soul enters there, it is as if scales fall from its eyes, and its gaze is intuitively raised toward the sun that dazzles it. It sees, in this light, the splendor to which divine love has destined it, taking it from nothingness. It becomes aware of the unfathomable riches it has been destined to possess since its origin by creative love. But it spent its life here with its eyes focused on the earth and its false attractions: it lived as a prisoner of the world and its fleeting lights, blinded by sin to the transparency of divine love. When it opens its eyes, they are too sensitive to sustain such splendor and perfection; thus the soul undergoes an intense suffering. Blinded in the very center of light, the soul feels as if rays of fire were passing through its head. At the same time, it is recollected in a great silence of love and a manifest gratitude that purifies the tumult of the world—the world to which it gave too much importance, delighting in it and making its ears deaf to perceive and savor the Word of God.

This silence of death is very painful to them, habituated as they are to moving in the clamor of the world. Their wounded hearing wants to hear, but they don't perceive anything, which produces a torturing anguish. The soul is waiting for God. The soul—which is agitated and moves in every direction, finding no rest in creatures and always seeking it elsewhere, away from its interior—sees itself here immobilized and paralyzed by desire for the One who attracts it, and it is impetuously drawn out of itself and held back by the weight of sin and its imperfections. It is a tearing apart of its whole being, because now it feels itself inserted in Christ crucified, to whom it should be totally conformed, letting itself be molded by the will of the Father, in the furnace of his crucified Son. It cannot be freed from the punishment of purgatory until the Father recognizes in it the face of the one who alone can incline toward mercy: the crucified Jesus.

Consumed by hunger, it cannot satisfy itself other than with its desire. Feeling an inextinguishable thirst, its drink consists only of its bitter tears, which cannot extinguish its thirst. But in that torturing hunger and thirst, it finds the will of God, its only food in the purgatory of divine love. The soul, which had constantly distanced itself from God and from itself, losing itself in creatures, is now held in its interior with only the gaze that the all powerful and infinite mercy of God fixes upon it. And only in the painful splendor of this mercy is it able to see the effects that are produced in the innermost part of its being: interior dislocation and the most terrible annihilation and dullness, similar to the spasms that a sick body might feel.

The soul is totally separated from every creature and only encounters in its own misery saturated with pain what the state of a creature is: it knows and experiences now that it is a creature that came from the loving hand of God, and humiliation and helplessness are the price of this knowledge. It wants to run toward him, touch him, apprehend him, yet it finds itself retained in itself, beneath the divine hand that holds it bowed down, and it wants nothing more than to be under that powerful hand.

It has left everything which is not God, ignoring whether anything other than him exists, and it doesn't perceive him other than indirectly, as if in a mirror of fire which it neither wants to nor can pass through.

IN THE SWEETNESS OF THE CLOSENESS OF MARY

Evening prayer. My soul felt itself filled with softness. It was as if the Virgin Mary took my heart into hers in an ineffable peace and sweetness. At the end of my prayer, she appeared to me like a great light above a fire, in which I recognized purgatory. Our Lady was standing with her hands extended toward the fire; waves of light descended from her heart to her fingers and were poured in an abundant rain on purgatory. She prayed, smiling with an indescribable tenderness. Purgatory opened up to my gaze, and I contemplated in the flames some souls who raised their hands toward the Mother of God, praying with confidence and receiving like a refreshing downpour the waves of rays of light that flowed from the heart and hands of Mary. Among them I recognized a girl who had been commended to my prayer because she was affected by a grave sickness and suffering greatly. The Blessed Virgin had told me:

> *My child, I will not cure her, because my Divine Son wants her close to him: he awaits her in heaven . . .*

That soul was in purgatory. After the impression of this surprise, I began to pray for her. She turned then a little, and without ceasing to look at Our Lady, said to me:

Yes, it is me; I have departed from earth.

The Blessed Virgin came yesterday to seek me. She had already come on other occasions to console me, smile at me, and encourage me.

My final days on earth were spent in the sweetness of intimacy with Mary. And you now see that I am saved!

I don't cease to thank God and to glorify him: I will sing his mercies forever! I died young, but I am saved. The Blessed Virgin helped me a lot because everything was very hard, but she taught me to forget myself for Jesus and for our brothers and sisters.

Now I never cease to glorify God and give him thanks for the incomparable gift of his Mother, who is so compassionate. Pray for me, if God allows this, and for my parents, so that they will be strong and not lose the faith and will glorify God in all things.

Then everything disappeared, and I felt a gentle joy. In three or four days a letter arrived that confirmed her death.

DRUNK WITH HOPE

Everything is very calm. This winter night I offered our Lord the peace that completely surrounded and inundated my soul. I prayed, and my guardian angel appeared on the stairs of the altar. He prostrated himself before the tabernacle, came silently toward me, and said softly:

Look, and pray for this soul . . .

I looked into a sea of fire, which suddenly appeared before my eyes, and I saw numerous souls in purgatory,

169

among whom I recognized a young woman who had died very recently. She looked at me kindly, extended her hands, and said:

May the peace of Jesus and the sweetness of Mary be in your soul!

As you can see, I am still in purgatory. I have come to ask you to pray for me. Our Lord has allowed me to take this step. Don't be sad to see me still here—pray and give thanks to God. Here we are drunk with hope: We burn in the fire of divine love and are drawn to him. It is a great fire, but we are patient and happy. I don't know if I will spend much time in purgatory, but it's not a great concern for me; I don't think about it. Our only concern is to glorify God, and I've come to you to invite you to pray for us, and thus to glorify the divine love.

Sing to the infinite mercy of God, uniting your prayer to ours, and pray without ceasing for us as we pray for you.

The soul disappeared from my interior gaze; the fire died down, and my angel concluded:

Yes, my child, you have to pray; to pray is to love. Prayer is the manifestation of your love of God and these holy souls. She is in what is called the ante-chamber of paradise. The offering to God of her great sufferings during her agony merited for her great graces of conversion, not only for her, but also for many souls: she was purified in her suffering and her purgatory will not be long.

The angel disappeared, leaving my soul in a gentle peace.

I HAVE BEEN SAVED BECAUSE I WAS GOOD

This first day of the year, the Solemnity of the Mother of God, has been overshadowed by a very painful death, which touched me closely. The Most Blessed Virgin poured a great peace on my soul, saying to my heart:

> *I am a mother, I am your mother, the mother of all of you, and I have you in my motherly heart.*

After Holy Mass, our Lord showed me my deceased one on a kind of coffin surrounded by flames. I had already had the grace of contemplating him on the two preceding days, but he had been lying down, covered by a shroud. I could see him, but he could not see me. I needed to pray. At that moment he stood up and extended his arms with a kind of restrained and melancholy joy. I, who could not control my tears, could not speak or make a gesture. My guardian angel was next to us, with his hand on my arm. He made the Sign of the Cross, which the dead person accepted with recollection. Then I also extended my hands toward him, and he said:

> *Let us give thanks to God!*
> *His mercy is infinite.*
> *You see, I am saved! Rejoice—I am saved!*
> *Rejoice—I am saved!*

As I was weeping without saying anything, he seemed to become sad, and then he scolded me with a certain severity:

Do not cry! You should be the strength of our relatives: You should assist and console them, surround them with a greater tenderness, showing them all the love that I have for them, which now they can no longer perceive. Yes, it is necessary for you to be their strength.

I answered with dismay: "How can I be their strength? Ask God to help them! I want to cry; I need to make reparation." My angel was serious: he squeezed my arm. The dead person turned to urge me again severely:

Do not weep! Your tears increase my suffering and deprive me of your consolation. Here we cannot merit, and your resignation and joy are meritorious to me: you can offer your merits for us! Don't you know that we are waiting for your prayers and acts of love? The smallest prayer is a glass of fresh water for a person dying of thirst in the desert.

Even a small fleeting thought is a light breeze in this burning desert, the fire of love that burns us. . . . If you only knew! I was saved because I was good. Our Lord preserved me from pride, egoism, and lies. But what makes me suffer here is my forgetting to seek him and wasting time.

Here I have discovered the world of infinite love, and this eases my suffering. Yes, I was good, but God is much more good to me. I have to discover, adore, and love his goodness.

You have to be a strong and good soul. Tell everyone that they should be good. Deus est caritas; sit caritas in vobis.[11]

---

[11] God is love; may his love be in all of you.

Praying for us is an obligation and a duty of charity toward God, whom you glorify, and toward us, who burn with the desire to contemplate him. It is the souls in purgatory that you alleviate and assist. Do you know that prayer for the souls in purgatory is one of your contributions to the unity of the Mystical Body? Ut unum sint! That we may all be one in him . . .

He became quiet and looked at me gently, and my soul was comforted. He opened his arms and, with a happy look toward heaven, said:

I have discovered the wonders of infinite love! Love has called me, I have been imprisoned by love, and now I am going toward love.
"Lord, all my longing is known to thee, my sighing is not hidden from thee!"[12]
As you see me in this moment, I will end by telling you: "Wait for the Lord; be strong, and let your heart take courage; yes, wait for the Lord!" [13]

MAY PRAYER BE THE INSTRUMENT OF UNITY

These last few days have been a trial: A young father, recently deceased, is buried. The family gathers, and their suffering is interiorized and purified little by little. After Mass, during the thanksgiving, I see the deceased near the altar surrounded by dim flames. I make the Sign of the Cross, and he then turns toward me, saying:

---

[12] Psalm 38:9.
[13] Psalm 27:14

Let us give thanks to God! Eternal goodness!
   *Do you know that I have seen the Most Blessed
Virgin? She is the Mother of goodness; she came to
me to bring me flowers.*

In the face of my surprise and joy, he smiled and
continued:

Yes, the flowers are a symbol of your prayers for me.
   *I have received suffrages from many people,
many of them unknown to me. Some of your
friends are praying for me, and I for my part am
praying for them, especially for the priests and
religious.*
   *Here we pray for the Church militant and for
all your intentions when God shows them to us,
but it doesn't seem to be always necessary. For us
it is a great consolation. This is a world of reparation. . . . We pray for the extension of the kingdom of God, for the coming of his kingdom of love
and peace, for the conversion of poor sinners, and
for the sanctification of souls.*
   *May prayer be an instrument of unity between
heaven, purgatory, and earth!*

My soul, filled with joy, wanted to ask other things, but
he looked at me and spoke to me again, this time sternly:

Don't forget that we are suffering very much.
   *In spite of everything, I have a particular
anguish because a movement is attracting me
toward the divine love, which is advancing, and*

I still am not able to follow it any further than within the limits of my present state. But I love this suffering, and I don't aspire to anything except God.

I tell him that I am sorry for him. He rose with an expression of nostalgic joy and, looking toward heaven, said:

God is good, so good, so good! And unfortunately they don't know it; they don't want to know.

It doesn't bother me to stay here for a long time in purgatory, if I have the consolation of being able to consecrate myself to him.

While this soul was speaking to me, he took holy water, presented it in the hollow of his hands, and said to me:

This procures great relief to us; you must not forget the sacramentals. I think that when I entered a church, I never forgot to take holy water, sometimes with a distracted gesture . . . because I was careless of practicing religion below. I now have to be almost constantly in a church near the altar, or beneath the altar when God allows it. There I receive abundant consolations through the application of all of the graces of the Most Blessed Sacrament.

But sometimes I see myself deprived of this because of my mediocre fervor. What comforts me is that Masses are said for the souls in purgatory; not only for me, but for all of us. For God receives your prayers and hands them over to his Holy

Mother, entrusting to her their application to the
souls in purgatory. You know that Mary Immacu-
late is the Mother of Goodness and always disposed
to do the most holy will of God, always receptive
to the effusions of his eternal goodness. She is the
instrument of the designs of God, who fulfills them
perfectly with so much goodness! One of the old
and deep treasures of the family is having Marian
devotion—never forget that!

My soul is filled with this luminous teaching, and I give
thanks to God, praying for this soul, who concludes thus:

Do you know that the angels come to see us? They
comfort us with their canticles; they publish with-
out ceasing the glory of God and honor his king-
dom with love and respect. This inflames our love
and increases our desire. We unite ourselves with
appreciation to their continual praise.
At times the Blessed Virgin turns to them,
asking them to send prayers that they bring to us
themselves as refreshing tides that alleviate us. And
when I see the angels, their beauty and perfection,
there increases in me the desire to see God, the
fountain of all good. In them is reflected the glory
and beauty of God, and this is a great consolation
for us.

And once more he was lost in this kind of ecstasy that
made him turn his eyes to heaven with an unspeakable joy.
After looking at me once more, he disappeared from my
view, leaving my soul consoled and happy.

MY ALMSGIVING SAVED ME

While praying in my room, I saw a kind of fiery whirlwind appear before me, in which there was a man I had known for many years. He died over twenty-five years ago. When I recognized him, I was surprised and felt a kind of consternation. Was this an illusion or a diabolical subterfuge? I made the Sign of the Cross, and peace invaded my soul. Then I asked this man if he would like to repeat the words "Jesus, Mary, and Joseph, I love you," and he did so.

This man had had a terrible reputation. He was not a believer, and he despised religion. They called him a libertine, unscrupulous, incapable of a good action, hard on his employees and his family, a gambler—in short, he was charged with all kinds of sins. He died in an accident, without having had time to receive the sacraments, and in a small town, tongues start wagging quickly. Many comments were made about his death and the probability of his eternal damnation. Unthinkingly, I had contributed to the spreading of those opinions, although seeing him in purgatory greatly consoled me. He looked at me, and I smiled at him and prayed for him, and then he exclaimed:

Thank you, my child, thank you!

If God allows me to show myself here, it is to alleviate my punishment and allow me to be consoled after so long a time. No one prays for me in my family; those closest to me have forgotten me. I have experienced a terrible purgatory, which was merited by my innumerable sins, but I was saved, as you see.

I felt happy to see him thus, and he continued:

Do you know what saved me?
It was the alms I gave—the frequent help I
gave to so many needy people—and many of those
good persons whom I assisted have prayed and
are praying for me without knowing that I am the
one who sent them that help, for I did it in secret,
anonymously. Now you see that you should never
judge anyone, nor trust appearances.
Would you like to pray for me and ask my chil-
dren to pray for me? This would glorify God and
hasten my liberation.

I promised him to do this, and he showed his joy. He made the Sign of the Cross and quickly disappeared. I was left meditating on his words.

THE MOST BLESSED VIRGIN COMES TO LIBERATE SOULS FROM PURGATORY

On this Feast of the Presentation of the Virgin Mary, I prolonged my thanksgiving to thank our Lord for his gift of his most holy Mother. I asked that he dispose my soul for the action of the Holy Spirit so that it too would be worthy of being presented to his Father, and I surrendered myself unreservedly to the loving will of the Blessed Trinity. With these considerations, my soul was recollected in God. I found myself full of peace.

After this there was a light, and in it I saw the Mother of God surrounded by a multitude of angels and blessed souls who descended to purgatory to bring consolation and love. St. Michael preceded them. A refreshing dew descended from Mary's heart and her hands and fell like rain on all of purgatory.

The Most Blessed Mother of God thus poured out graces, consolation, and hope. Afterward, she rose to heaven with many souls freed through her intercession. I saw hundreds of persons entering into the glory of God, and it was as if all of paradise resounded with a clamor of joy and festive songs. Among the souls freed on the occasion of this feast, I saw some of those who had implored me for prayers.

A TRIP TO HEAVEN AND PRAYER FOR THE HOLY SOULS

During the whole day the holy souls in purgatory were present. I saw multitudes, silent and praying, who extended their arms in a gesture of supplication. I was upset by this continual vision that was superimposed like a watermark over all the thousands of souls I saw who passes by asking for prayers. In the evening my guardian angel told me very seriously:

> They are coming toward you, begging for love and asking for prayer.

At nightfall, when I was finishing my prayers, I saw a great number of these souls coming toward me, moaning and clinging to my clothes. Thus they showed me how much these souls are forgotten, how alone they are. . . . The first of November has just passed, and during this month, many of the faithful and even priests no longer think of these souls. They don't pray much for them, except occasionally. And, nevertheless, these good souls, sure of their eternal salvation, are totally forgetful of themselves for the sole glory of God.[14] They are so full of gratitude toward us when they reach the happiness of heaven!

Once more I would like to remind you how much (more than anything!) they are consoled by the Holy Sacrifice of the Mass. We have to offer Masses and suffrages for their intention. And also the Holy Rosary—meditating on the mysteries and adding to each decade a Hail Mary for the souls in purgatory. We have a lot to learn from them: to suffer, be silent, pray, love, and adore. To dedicate oneself totally to the pure will of God.

Early this morning my guardian angel asked me to pray for the souls in purgatory. I did this through the liturgical texts of the day. We are all "beloved sons" in the Divine Son crucified and glorified.

During the day the vision of the suffering souls did not cease for an instant, except during one part of the Mass and in the course of the prayer. It was a vision that superimposed itself on all my activities. I don't know whether it

---

[14] "The souls in purgatory are impeccable, and cannot have the slightest movement of impatience, nor commit the slightest imperfection. They love God more than themselves and any other thing, with a perfect and disinterested love. They are consoled by the angels. They are assured of salvation. Their very great bitterness is within a profound peace. It is a kind of hell, as far as pain is concerned, but a paradise in regard to the sweetness which charity pours into their heart—a charity that is stronger than death. A happy state, more desired than felt, because those flames are of love and charity!" (Father Camus, "El Espiritu de San Francisco de Sales," in Joubert and Cristiani "Les plus beaux texts," 203).

was an imaginary vision or a corporal one, but this is really unimportant. Often these souls pass in front of me as a multitude without saying anything or seeing anything, as though overwhelmed. At times some of them turn toward me and extend their hands silently, their eyes filled with tears. This is anguishing to see and costs me so much effort that at the end of the day, during evening prayer, I am in a state of total exhaustion.

Later that day I had a very comforting vision. Many souls were rising from purgatory to the plenitude of divine love, carried in the grace of Mary Immaculate to enter into the heavenly Jerusalem. It seems that every soul that finishes its purification is incorporated in the grace of Mary Immaculate, elevated in the light of her love, and in this way the soul is introduced into the glory of heaven. I saw this as a manifestation of the universal maternity of the Blessed Virgin, which extends over all her children. There is great jubilation in heaven when a soul arrives; it's a movement of joy that celebrates the encounter of the soul with God, and this encounter into the mystery of the divine mercy is extended to the whole of paradise in concentric circles. This made me think of the encounter of the father with his prodigal son.

FEAST OF THE PRESENTATION OF THE BLESSED VIRGIN IN THE TEMPLE

I was praying for the suffering souls, meditating on what I had seen the previous evening, when my soul was elevated to contemplate the Mother of God, who opened her Immaculate Heart to the holy souls of purgatory. I saw that maternal heart like a golden door through which great numbers of souls pass to enter into the Heart of Jesus, which is the heaven of most pure love. They had been liberated on this feast day from the pains that they had suffered until that moment. I saw how some of the saints of paradise sent down stairs of light, along which the souls climbed to elevate themselves above the place of purification. We here below, by our prayers, suffrages, and sacrifices, help free them from the weight which prevents them from climbing those stairs to enjoy the happiness of the elect.

The Blessed Virgin presented all the souls liberated on this day to her divine Son. She whispered in their hearts: "Do whatever he tells you." These holy souls are jubilant and questioning. Jesus shows them his pierced Heart and tells them: "Read in this Heart how much I love you and what you must do now and for eternity." The souls read with rapture: "Glory be to the Father, to the Son, and to the Holy Spirit for all eternity." There came forth from this divine Heart a liquid that extinguished thirst. They drank with joy and an extraordinary jubilation. My angel then told me: "They drink with long draughts and with the pure desire to love of the Trinity of God." I experienced an indescribable rapture seeing these marvels. Afterward everything disappeared, and I remained in the recollection of thanksgiving.

THEOLOGICAL NOTE
ON PURGATORY

From its origins, the Church, through its prayers and suffrages for the deceased, has clearly shown its faith in purgatory. Later, with wise cautiousness, it defined its doctrine in the Second Council of Lyon (1274), the Council of Florence (1438), and the Council of Trent (Twenty-Fifth Session, December 1563). Let us recall the broad lines of this doctrine, which is so luminous and consoling:

* In purgatory, the souls of the just pay their debt to divine justice, suffering purifying punishment. We point out, in the first place, that the purification of purgatory is not focused on the *fault*, but on its *punishment*. If God's pardon, granted to the repentant soul, erases the fault, it does not make the punishment disappear, then this is the means that man has to repair the disorder that his sins have occasioned. Here on earth the soul suffers punishment under the form of a voluntary and meritorious penance. In the other world it is under the form of an obligatory purification.

* According to the doctrine of the Church, there are two classes of punishments in purgatory. The principal one is the temporary privation of the vision of

God, accompanied by unheard of suffering. The soul burns with desire to see God, but it cannot attain him, because it did not expiate its sins sufficiently before death. The expiation ends, then, in purgatory, and it takes on a form of suffering that one cannot imagine here on earth. In purgatory there are other pains, called "pains of the senses," but the Church has never made a pronouncement about the exact nature of these pains. The object is to repair the disordered attachment to creatures.

• The pains of purgatory are not the same for all souls. They vary in duration and intensity according to the culpability of each one. The souls receive serenely the expiatory sufferings that God inflicts upon them. They do not seek anything except the glory of God, and they desire ardently to contemplate the One who is, from now on, their whole hope. In purgatory there reigns a great peace and joy, for the souls there have total certainty of their salvation, and they see their pain solely as a means of glorifying the sanctity of God and thus arriving at the glorious vision. The sufferings of purgatory are no longer meritorious, nor do they increase charity in the soul of the one who is suffering.

• The Church on earth can help through its suffrages the Church "which is being cleansed beyond the doors of death" (Cardinal Journet); they are united by one and the same love in Christ. This union creates the possibility of a communication of merits. The souls in purgatory, incapable of procuring for themselves the slightest alleviation, can thus take advantage of the works of expiation that the living carry out in their favor with the intention of paying their debts. These works of satisfaction have the value of expiation for the punishment of the holy souls, and it is God who regulates the application of suffrages for the dead according to his wisdom.

The Mass is the most efficacious help that the Church on earth (the Church militant) can provide to the souls being purified. Is not the Mass, in fact, the sacrifice offered by Jesus on the cross for the salvation of the world? Alms, prayers, and all forms of sacrifice are also means to help "our good friends who are suffering" (St. Margaret Mary).

• Purgatory will terminate in the final judgment. All souls destined to glory will have satisfied by then, in one form or another, divine justice.

The preceding content expresses what is essential in the teachings of the Church about the mystery of purgatory. We have to add that the Council of Florence did not define whether the souls in purgatory are purified by a real or a metaphorical fire. The common doctrine (at least in the Latin Church) considers the punishment of fire to be real, basing itself on the authority of St. Gregory Nazianzen and St. Gregory the Great. But the Church leaves the task of providing some light on other secondary questions to the theologians, such as: Where is purgatory found? Is venial sin forgiven at the moment of death or in the place of purification? Do the souls in purgatory pray for us?

For the souls of the just, purgatory is the state and place of suffering in which punishments are expiated that have not been satisfied in this world[1] (i.e., mortal and venial sins that are already forgiven). The venial sins are forgiven in terms of guilt, if they have not been forgiven during one's lifetime.[2]

The existence of purgatory is a truth of the faith. St. Thomas Aquinas did not hesitate to affirm that to deny purgatory is to speak against divine justice and commit an error against the faith.[3] This truth is based on an explicit teaching of Scripture about the judgment and the requirement of perfect purity to enter into heaven. If the term "purgatory" is not found in Scripture, the reality of what it represents is found in Judas Maccabeus, who would not have offered expiatory sacrifices in the Temple of Jerusalem for the soldiers of his army who died in combat if he had not believed in the possibility that the dead could be purified and expiate the consequences of their sins.[4]

[1] St. Thomas Aquinas, *Summa Theologica*, Supplement, q. 70 ter, a. 1.
[2] St. Thomas Aquinas, *Compendium*, Ch. 181.
[3] St. Thomas Aquinas, *Summa Theologica* IIIa, 70 bis. Art. 6.
[4] 2 Maccabees 12:38–45.

BIBLIOGRAPHY

I. The Magisterium

Tenth Council of Lyon, Fourth Session (July 6, 1274). Profession of Faith of Michael Palaeologus.

Council of Florence, Decree for the Greeks (July 6, 1439).

Bull *Exsurge Domine,* of Pope Leo X (June 14, 1520). Condemns certain erroneous propositions on purgatory.

The Council of Trent:

— Decree on Justification, session 6 (January 13, 1547).

— Doctrine on the Holy Sacrifice of the Mass, session 22 (September 17, 1562).

— Doctrine on Purgatory, session 25 (December 3-4, 1563).

Profession of Faith of Paul VI, June 20, 1968.

Letter on Some Questions Concerning Eschatology, Sacred Congregation for the Doctrine of the Faith, May 17, 1979.

Catechism of the Catholic Church, Association of Editors of the Catechism, 3rd ed., 1992.

II. Writings of the Saints

St. Augustine (431), *De Cura Gerenda pro Mortuis.* Bibliothèque Augustinienne, vol. 2, Desclée de Brouwer.

St. Thomas Aquinas (1274), *Summa Theologica,* Supplement, Questions 69–74.

St. Catherine of Genoa (1510):

— *Treatise on Purgatory*

— *Spiritual Dialogue*

St. John of the Cross (1591), *Spiritual Works.*

St. Veronica Giuliani, *Journal,* pages translated from her *Diario,* Gembloux: Duculot, 1931.

III. OTHER WORKS

Garrigou-Lagrange, O.P., Reginald. *Life Everlasting.* Charlotte, NC: TAN Books, 1952.

Joubert J. and Cristiani, L. *Les plus beaux texts sur l'audela.* Paris: La Colombe, 1950.

Journet, Cardinal Charles. *Le Purgatoire.* Études Religieuses.

Laurentin, René. *"Fonction et Statut des Aparitions,"* in *Vrais et Fausses Apparitions dans l'Église.* Paris: Lethielleux, 1976.